Auguste Sabatier

Outlines of a Philosophy of Religion

Based on Psychology and History

Auguste Sabatier

Outlines of a Philosophy of Religion
Based on Psychology and History

ISBN/EAN: 9783337071004

Printed in Europe, USA, Canada, Australia, Japan

Cover: Foto ©ninafisch / pixelio.de

More available books at **www.hansebooks.com**

Outlines of a Philosophy of Religion based on Psychology and History

By *Auguste Sabatier*
Dean of the Faculty of Protestant Theology, Paris

Authorised Translation by the Rev. T. A. Seed

LONDON
HODDER AND STOUGHTON
27 PATERNOSTER ROW
1897

CONTENTS

	PAGE
PREFACE	xi

BOOK I.—RELIGION

CHAPTER I

THE PSYCHOLOGICAL ORIGIN AND THE NATURE OF RELIGION

1. First Critical Reflections 3
2. Initial Contradiction of the Psychological Consciousness . 13
3. Religion the Prayer of the Heart . . . 27

CHAPTER II

Religion and Revelation

		PAGE
1.	The Mystery of the Religious Life	32
2.	Mythological Notion of Revelation	37
3.	Dogmatic Notion	44
4.	Psychological Notion	54
5.	Conclusion	64

CHAPTER III

Miracle and Inspiration

1.	The Notion of Miracle in Antiquity	69
2.	Miracle and Science: Miracle and Piety	76
3.	Religious Inspiration	85

CHAPTER IV

The Religious Development of Humanity

1.	The Social Element in Religion	91
2.	Progress in the Outward Forms of Religion	95
3.	Progress in the Representation of the Divine	102
4.	The History of Prayer	109
5.	Conclusion	115

BOOK II.—CHRISTIANITY

CHAPTER I

HEBRAISM, OR THE ORIGINS OF THE GOSPEL

		PAGE
1.	Prophetism	122
2.	The Dawn of the Gospel	126

CHAPTER II

THE ESSENCE OF CHRISTIANITY

1.	The Problem	135
2.	The Christian Principle	147
3.	The Gospel of Jesus	152
4.	A Necessary Distinction	164
5.	The Corruptions of the Christian Principle	169

CHAPTER III

THE GREAT HISTORICAL FORMS OF CHRISTIANITY

1.	The Evolution of the Christian Principle	177
2.	Jewish or Messianic Christianity	181
3.	Catholic Christianity	196
4.	Protestant Christianity	207
5.	Conclusion	222

BOOK III.—DOGMA

CHAPTER I

What is a Dogma?

	PAGE
1. Definition	229
2. Genesis of Dogma	232
3. The Rôle and the Religious Value of Dogma	239

CHAPTER II

The Life of Dogmas and their Historical Evolution

1. Three Prejudices	244
2. The Two Elements in Dogma	246
3. The Crisis of Dogma	253

CHAPTER III

The Science of Dogmas

1. Mixed Character of the Science of Dogmas	259
2. The Science of Dogmas and the Church	262
3. The Science of Dogmas and Philosophy	268

CHAPTER IV

CRITICAL THEORY OF RELIGIOUS KNOWLEDGE

		PAGE
1.	Antiquated Theories	277
2.	The Kantian Theory of Knowledge	282
3.	The Two Orders of Knowledge	294
4.	Subjectivity of Religious Knowledge	303
5.	Teleology	315
6.	Symbolism	322
7.	Conclusion	334

APPENDIX

Reply to Criticisms 345

PREFACE

THIS volume contains three parts which are related to each other as the three stories of one and the same edifice. The first treats of religion and its origin; the second of Christianity and its essence; the third of Dogma and its nature.

Proceeding thus from the general to the particular, from the elementary forms of religion to its highest form, passing afterwards from religious phenomena to religious doctrines, I have endeavoured to develop a series of connected and progressive views which I do not wish to be regarded as a system, but as the rigid application and the first results of the method of strictly psychological and historical observation that for years I have applied to this species of studies. In no domain is there a greater incoherence of ideas, a sharper conflict of feeling, or data more contradictory or, at all events, more difficult to reconcile. In no other is it more urgent to introduce a little sequence, clearness, harmony.

Our century, from the beginning, has had two great passions which still inflame and agitate its closing years. It has driven abreast the twofold worship of the scientific method and of the moral ideal ; but, so far from being able to unite them, it has pushed them to a point where they seem to contradict and exclude each other. Every serious soul feels itself to be inwardly divided ; it would fain conciliate its most generous aspirations, the two last motives for living and acting that still remain to it. Where but in a renovated conception of religion will this needed reconciliation be found ?

No one nowadays underestimates the social importance of the religious question. Philosophers, moralists, politicians, show themselves to be alive to it ; they see it dominating all others, whose solution, in the end, it may prevent or decide. But, singular contradiction ! the more zeal and the more decision these men manifest in handling the religious question in the social order, the more indifference or impotence they show in solving it for themselves both in their inner and their family life. . . . No one has the right to impose a doctrine or the presumption, surely, to dictate to others how they must direct their thought ; but a sincere and persuaded mind may tell how it has directed its own, and may set forth as an experience and a "document" the views at which it has arrived. . . .

The solidarity of minds has now become so great, the currents of ideas, like the currents in the atmosphere, move so quickly and create, in circumstances so different and so far apart, states of soul so similar that many who read these studies, and who are struggling with the same difficulties as those which have so long engaged the author's thoughts, may find both interest and profit in seeing how he has succeeded in satisfying himself. Those even who have never reflected on these questions, or have lightly turned from them because they deemed them insoluble, will not perhaps object to be directed to them by one who wishes, not to check their freedom of thought, but to stimulate them to exercise it. Who, at the close of his secret meditations, on the confines of his knowledge, at the end of his affections, of the joys he has tasted, of the trials he has endured, has not seen rising before him the religious question—I mean the mysterious problem of his destiny? Of all questions it is the most vital. Men may be turned from it for a time by manifold distractions and by a sense of powerlessness to solve the question, but it is impossible that they should not return to it. Has life a meaning? Is it worth living? Our efforts, have they an end? Our works and our thoughts, have they any permanent value to the universe? This problem, which one generation may evade, returns with the next. Each new recruit to the human race brings the problem along with him, because he wishes to live, and to live is to act, and all action requires a faith. It is of the young that I have thought while preparing these pages, and it is to them that I dedicate them.

To a generation that believed it could repose in Positivism in philosophy, utilitarianism in morals, and naturalism in art and poetry, has succeeded a generation that torments itself more than ever with the mystery of things, that is attracted by the ideal, that dreams of social fraternity, of self-renunciation, of devotion to the little, to the miserable, to the oppressed—devotion like the heroism of Christian love. Hence what has been called the renaissance of Idealism, the return, *i.e.*, to general ideas, to faith in the invisible, to the taste for symbols, and to those longings, as confused as they are ardent, to discover a religion or to return to the religion their fathers have disdained. Our young people, it seems to me, are pushing bravely forward, marching between two high walls:

on the one side modern science with its rigorous methods which it is no longer possible to ignore or to avoid; on the other, the dogmas and the customs of the religious institutions in which they were reared, and to which they would, but cannot, sincerely return. The sages who have led them hitherto point to the *impasse* they have reached, and bid them take a part,—either for science against religion, or for religion against science. They hesitate, with reason, in face of this alarming alternative. Must we then choose between pious ignorance and bare knowledge? Must we either continue to live a moral life belied by science, or set up a theory of things which our consciences condemn? Is there no issue to the dark and narrow valley which our anxious youth traverse? I think there is. I think I have caught glimpses of a steep and narrow path that leads to wide and shining table-lands above. Indeed I have ascended in the footsteps of some others, and I signal in my turn to younger, braver pioneers who, in course of time, will make a broader, safer road, along which all the caravan may pass.

BOOK FIRST

RELIGION

CHAPTER I

ON THE PSYCHOLOGICAL ORIGIN, AND ON THE NATURE OF RELIGION

1. *First Critical Reflections*

WHY am I religious? Because I cannot help it: it is a moral necessity of my being. They tell me it is a matter of heredity, of education, of temperament. I have often said so to myself. But that explanation simply puts the problem further back; it does not solve it.

The necessity which I experience in my individual life I find to be still more invincible in the collective life of humanity. Humanity is not less incurably religious than I am. The cults it has espoused and abandoned have deceived it in vain; in vain has the criticism of savants and philosophers shattered its dogmas and mythologies; in vain has religion left such tracks of blood and fire throughout the annals of humanity; it has survived all change, all revolution, all stages of culture and progress. Cut down a thousand times, the ancient stem has always sent new branches forth. Whence comes this indestructible vitality? What is the cause of the universality and perpetuity of religion?

Before entering upon this question it will be necessary to remove a fruitful cause of error with respect to the essence and origin of the religious sense, especially among the peoples of Latin extraction. This cause lies in the very word *religion*. It very badly designates the psychological phenomenon to be studied; it envelops it in accessory and even in alien ideas, which blind and mislead half-educated men. The word comes to us from the least religious of the peoples of the world. It has no synonym or equivalent in the language of the ancient Hebrews, or in that of the Greeks, the Germans, the Celts, or the Hindus, the human families which, in the religious order, have been the most original and the most creative. It was Rome that imposed the word upon us along with her language, her genius, and her institutions.

The first Christians were not acquainted with it. It is absent from the New Testament. When, in the third century, it enters into Christian speech, it no doubt undergoes a sort of baptism, and seems to cover a meaning more in conformity with the spirit of the Gospel. Lactantius defines religion as "the link which unites man to God." But in the ancient Roman writers the word never had this profound and mystical meaning. Instead of marking the inward and subjective side of religion, and signalising it as a phenomenon of the life of the soul, it defined religion by the outside, as a tradition of rites, and as a social institution bequeathed by ancestors. The Christian baptism through which the word passed did not efface this ancient Roman stamp. To the majority, even now, religion is hardly anything more than a series of traditional rites, supernatural beliefs, political institutions; it is a Church in possession of divine sacraments, constituted by a sacerdotal hierarchy, for the discipline and government of souls. Such is the form under which the genius of Rome conceived and realised Christianity in the Western world; and the fascination that this political and social conception of religion still exercises is so great that minds the most enlightened know no better than to agree with M. Brunetière, who, when wishing to set forth the superiority of Catholicism to Protestantism, confines himself, like Bossuet, to praising it as a perfect model of government.

By a sort of logical necessity, whenever and wherever this political conception of religion has predominated, an analogous explanation of its origin has always arisen. It is natural that men should have applied to it the ancient juridical adage: *is fecit cui prodest.* Religion admirably serves to govern the peoples; therefore it was originally invented for that purpose. It was the work of priests and chiefs who wished by means of it to strengthen and to ratify their authority. So reason the Romans in the days of Cicero and the philosophers of the eighteenth century. And there is some foundation for their arguments. Religion has often been utilised by politics: pious frauds are to be found in all the cults. But what then? What do the facts prove? It is not the pious fraud that produces the religion; it is the religion that gives occasion and opportunity to pious frauds. Without religion there would have been no pious frauds. When I hear it said, "Priests made religion," I simply ask, "And who, pray, made the priests?" In order to create a priesthood, and in order that that invention should find general acceptance with the people that were to be subject to it, must there not have been already in the hearts of men a religious sentiment that would clothe the institution with a sacred character? The terms must be reversed: it is not priesthood that explains religion, but religion that explains priesthood.

The theory propounded by Positivism is profounder and more serious. Religion, which dates from the earliest ages, can only have been a first attempt at an explanation of the extraordinary phenomena by which man in his ignorance was astonished and frightened. It is the beginning of the childish form of science, which, in course of time, would naturally give place to higher and more rigorous forms. Children and savages animate all things round about them with a psychical life; they see particular wills behind every phenomenon that excites their hope or fear. Thus the imagination of primitive man peopled the universe with an infinite number of spirits, good and evil, whose mysterious action made itself felt at every moment of their destiny. A while ago we had the explanation of religion by priesthood; now we have the explanation by mythology. But it is the same vicious circle: it is an insufficient psychology once more mistaking the effect for the cause.

To conceive of religion as a species of knowledge is an error not less grave than to represent it as a sort of political institution. No doubt religious faith is always accompanied by knowledge, but this intellectual element, however indispensable, so far from being the basis and the substance of religion, varies continually at all the epochs of religious evolution. Doctrinal formulas and liturgies are means of expression and of education, of which religion avails itself, but which it can exchange for others after each philosophical crisis. Rites and beliefs become obliterated or die out; religion possesses a power of perpetual resurrection, whose principle cannot be exhausted in any external form or in any dogmatic idea.

Comte's theory of the three stages through which human thought has passed is well known: the theological stage of primitive times, the metaphysical stage in the Middle Ages, the positive or scientific stage of modern times. If knowledge were the essence of religion, one could easily understand the logical course of this evolution, an inferior form of knowledge being condemned to disappear before a superior form. The proof that it is nothing of the kind is the fact that religion does not cease to reappear at all epochs and in the most widely different conditions of culture. The three stages are not successive but simultaneous; they do not correspond to three periods of history, but to three permanent needs of the human soul. You find them combined in various degrees in antiquity, in Socrates, Plato, and Aristotle; in modern times, in Descartes, Pascal, Leibniz, Kant, Claude Bernard, and Pasteur. The more science progresses and becomes conscious of its true method and of its limits, the more does it become distinguished from philosophy and religion. Scientific research, exclusively devoted to the determination of phenomena and of their conditions in time and space, is one thing; the philosophic need of comprehending the universe as an intelligible whole, and of explaining all that exists by a principle of sufficient reason, is another and a different thing; and, lastly, differing from both, is the religious need which, rightly understood, is but a manifestation, in the moral order, of the instinct of every being to persevere in being. Why may not these divers tendencies of soul, coexisting always and everywhere, manifest themselves simultaneously and on parallel lines?

We need not go beyond the Positivists themselves for examples and proofs of this persistence of the religious sentiment. Comte, Spencer, and Littré may be called as witnesses. The founder of Positivism, who had predicted the fatal extinction of the disposition to religion in the human soul, crowned his system and ended his career by founding a new religion, clumsily copied from the sacerdotal organisation and the ritual practices of Roman Catholicism. There actually exists a Positivist Church, with a calendar of saints, with relics and anniversaries, with a catechism, and with a high priest not less infallible than the one at Rome. A few disciples, scandalised by this supreme temptation of the master, desired to excuse him by declaring that he had gone mad. It was a mistake. The fact is that, arriving at the construction of a Positive Sociology, Comte comprehended the *rôle* of the religious instinct and of religious feeling in the life of peoples, and he believed that he would only be able to cement the edifice of society in the future by religion. It is said that those who have been amputated sometimes feel sharp twitches in the limbs they have lost. Comte and his disciples have experienced something similar. Nature, with her usual irony, has avenged herself on them for the violence they have done to her.

Of Herbert Spencer not much need be said; everybody knows that the *Unknowable* in his system has become a sort of undetermined and unconscious force, eluding every effort of the mind to grasp it, but remaining, none the less, the cause explaining evolution, and the source profound whence all things flow. Under different names, do we not recognise the First Cause of the philosophers, and the image, half-effaced, of the God of believers? Need we be surprised that the English thinker pronounces religion to be eternal? that he finally reduces the mental life of man to these two essential and primordial activities—the scientific activity which pursues the knowledge of phenomena and their transformation, and religious activity delivering itself up to mystical contemplation and to silent adoration of universal being?

The example of Littré is more touching still. I remember reading a sublime page in one of his works, in which the savant, after running through the *terra firma* of positive knowledge, reaches its utmost limit, and, seating himself on the extremest promontory, sees himself surrounded by the mystery of the unknowable, as by an infinite ocean. He has neither barque, nor sails, nor compass wherewith to explore this boundless sea; nevertheless, he stands there gazing into it; he contemplates it; he meditates in presence of this vast unknown, and finally abandons himself to a movement of adoration and of confidence which renews his mental vigour and which fills his heart with peace. What is this, I ask, but a sudden outburst of religious feeling which positive science, so far from extinguishing, has only served to deepen and accentuate? And since we have here the religion of the unknowable, is it not evident that religion is not necessarily knowledge?

I now come to a third explanation which, older than either of the others, will bring us nearer to the end at which we aim. "It is fear," says a Latin poet, "that engenders the gods." There is a sense in which this is true. It cannot be doubted that religion was at first awakened in the heart of man under the impress of the terror caused by the disordered and destructive forces of primitive Nature. Thrown naked and disarmed on the barely-cooled planet, walking tremblingly upon a soil that quaked beneath his tread, his would be a state of misery and distress which filled his heart with an infinite terror. But the explanation needs completing. In itself and of itself, fear is not religious; it paralyses, crushes, stuns. In order that it may become religiously fruitful, it is necessary that, from the outset, it should be mixed with an opposite sentiment, an impulse of hope; it is necessary that man, the prey of fear, should conceive, in some way or other, the possibility of surmounting it—that is to say that he should find above him some help, some succour, by which to confront the dangers which threaten him. Fear only gives birth to religion in man because it awakens hope and calls forth prayer—prayer that opens an issue to human distress. There is that amount of truth in the ancient hypothesis. It brings us near the source we are seeking, for it places us on the practical arena of life, and not in the theoretical region of science. The question man puts to himself in religion is always a question of salvation, and if he seems sometimes to be pursuing in it the enigma of the universe, it is only that he may solve the enigma of his life. And now we must press nearer to the problem. We must ascertain out of what fundamental contradiction the religious feeling arises. We may reach it by a mental analysis that every one can follow, and verify the more easily inasmuch as it is always in course of reconstruction, by noting our own experiences.

2. *Initial Contradiction of the Psychological Consciousness*

What is man? Externally he does not differ much from the higher animals, the series of which seems to have been closed by his appearance on our planet. His physical organism is composed of the same elements, acting according to the same laws; and of the same organs, performing analogous functions. It is by the incomparable development of his mental life that man is distinguished, and little by little disengages himself from animality. Phenomena and laws of a new kind now make their appearance. The mysterious life of the spirit, emerging from the physical life, unfolds itself gradually like a divine flower, and gives the world, for us, its meaning and its loveliness. The region of the true, the beautiful, the good, is opened up to consciousness; the moral world is constituted as a higher order to which man belongs. It is these moral laws, capable of dominating physical laws and bending them to higher ends that, in the human animal, realise and constitute humanity. Man is only man in so far as he obeys them, and such is the point of transition that he occupies between two worlds, such the necessity of the crisis by which he must disengage himself from material animality, that, if he does not rise above the brute, he necessarily, by the very perversion of his higher life, falls beneath him.

From the beginning, physical life implies a double movement: a movement inward from the outside to the centre of the ego, and a movement outward from the centre to the circumference. The first represents the action of external things upon the ego by sensation (passivity); the second, the reaction of the ego upon things by the will (activity). This internal flux and reflux is the whole mental life. From this point we shall soon perceive the initial contradiction in which this life is formed, and in which it goes on developing itself continually. The passive side and the active side of the life of the mind are not harmonious. Sensation crushes the will. The activity, the free expansion of the ego, its desires to extend and aggrandise itself are checked and crushed by the weight of the world, which on every side is pressing in upon it. Springing up from the centre, the wave of life breaks itself inevitably on the rocks of outward things. This perpetual collision, this conflict of the ego and the universe,—this is the primary cause and origin of all pain. Thus thrown back upon itself, the activity of the ego returns upon the centre and heats it like the axle of a wheel in motion. Sparks soon fly, and the inner life of the ego is lit up. This is *consciousness*. Brought back by painful sensations and by repeated failure of its efforts from the outside, the ego begins to reflect upon itself; it doubles itself and knows itself; soon it judges itself; it separates itself from the organism with which at first it confounded itself; it opposes itself to itself, as if there were really in itself two *beings*, an ideal ego and an empirical ego. Hence comes its torment, its struggles, its remorse, but also the impulse ever renewed, the indefinite progress of its spiritual life, of which each moment seems to be but a degree from which it ought to rise to a stage still higher.

May we not here foresee the divine purpose of pain? Without it, it would seem as if the life of the spirit could not have arisen out of physical life. All births are painful. Consciousness, like every other child, was born in tears. The child of pain, it can only be developed by pain. Where do you find intelligence the most refined, consciousness the keenest, inner life the most intense, if not amongst the human beings whose external activities have been repressed by sickness or by some limitation in their social position? How else will you explain the *Pensées* of Pascal or of Maine de Biran, or the *Journal* of Amiel? Whence comes that extraordinary development of consciousness of which we are all aware in men like these, unless it be that they feel more profoundly than others that radical contradiction which constitutes at once the misery and the grandeur of human destiny?

Continue this observation; follow each of our faculties in its progressive expansion. Starting from a contradiction without which they would not exist, you see them all end in a contradiction in which they seem to perish, so that that which has engendered consciousness seems as if it must destroy it. Everywhere the same discouraging antinomy. Man cannot know himself without knowing himself to be limited. But he cannot feel these fatal limitations without going beyond them in thought and by desire, so that he is never satisfied with what he possesses, and cannot be happy except with that which he cannot attain. I desire to know; my labouring intellect is athirst to comprehend and understand, and its first discoveries enchant it. But, alas, my head soon runs itself against the wall of mystery. Not only are there things it does not know, but there are things which it knows for a certainty that it will never be able to know. How can a man jump off his own shadow, or stand on his own shoulders, to look over the impassable wall? That all which is intelligible to us is real, I grant; but is all that is real intelligible to us? And then what becomes my knowledge save a melancholy feeling of ignorance that knows itself to be such? The same contradiction in my faculty for enjoyment. As my seeming knowledge changed into its opposite, so now I see pleasure and happiness changing into pain and sorrow. Let the superficial and the vulgar lay on fate or things the blame of their deceptions and of their inability to be happy; as for me, I can only blame the inner constitution of my being. It is as the result of that very constitution that enjoyment bears within itself the cause of its own exhaustion, that pleasure is changed into disgust, and that pain is born of all voluptuousness. Pessimism is in the right; for it is proved by an experience only too long-lived that the only result of happiness exclusively pursued is an increase of the capacity for suffering. Need I speak of moral activity? I desire to do good, but "evil is present with me." I do not do that which I approve, and I do not approve that which I do: I feel myself free in my will, and I am enslaved in action. The more effort I make towards an ideal righteousness, the more that ideal, which I never reach, constitutes me a sinner and strengthens in me the consciousness of sin; so that here again, and here especially, the final result of my search is the opposite of that which I set out to seek.

Whence shall deliverance come? How shall I solve this contradiction of my being which makes me at the same time live and die? To free man from the miseries and limitations of his nature men count upon the progress of science and the amelioration of the conditions of his life. But who does not see that here is a new source of despair? How can we forget that, so far from attenuating it, science in its progress aggravates and renders mortal the original condition of life? To make a discovery, to explain a new phenomenon, what is this but to add another link to the causal and necessary network which science weaves and spreads over things? To put sequence, order, and stability into the world, is not this, for science, to put necessity into it, and to make necessity the sovereign ruler of the world? Science, in the strict sense of the word, is determinist. But then, prolong this progress of science indefinitely; multiply it by ten, by a hundred, a thousand; what do you do but multiply proportionately the weight of universal determinism beneath which our soul groans and ceases to strive? We should then end in the still more tragic contradiction—between science and conscience, physical laws and moral laws, action and reflection. The more the one enlarges and triumphs the vainer seems the other. Hence that philosophical dualism in which modern thought ends—a science which cannot engender an acknowledged morality, and a morality which cannot be the object of positive science. We touch the cause of that strange malady *le mal du siècle*, a sort of internal consumption by which all cultivated minds are more or less affected. It is an intestine war which arms the human ego against itself and dries up all the springs of life. The more one reflects on the reasons that may be urged in favour of living and acting, the less capable one is of effort and of action. Clearness of thought is in inverse proportion to the energy of the will. The Pessimists tell us that if we were fully and perfectly conscious we should lose the will to act, and even the desire to be. And which of us is not more or less of a Pessimist nowadays? Who does not complain of "the weary weight of all this unintelligible world"? Who does not feel his weakness and the pressure of external things? Who has not marked that union now become almost habitual of frivolity of character and intellectual culture the most perfect and refined? That sad monotone which comes to us on every wind, from the latest volume of philosophy, from the most popular novel, from the most successful play,—what is it but the melancholy sigh of a life that seems to be ready to expire, of a world that seems about to disappear. Must one give up thinking then if he would retain the courage to live, and resign himself to death in order to preserve the right to think?

From this feeling of distress, from this initial contradiction of the inner life of man, religion springs. It is the rent in the rock through which the living and life-giving waters flow. Not that religion brings a theoretical solution to the problem. The issue it opens and proposes to us is pre-eminently practical. It does not save us by adding to our knowledge, but by a return to the very principle on which our being depends, and by a moral act of confidence in the origin and aim of life. At the same time this saving act is not an arbitrary one; it springs from a necessity. Faith in life both is and acts like the instinct of conservation in the physical world. It is a higher form of that instinct. Blind and fatal in organisms, in the moral life it is accompanied by consciousness and by reflective will, and, thus transformed, it appears under the guise of religion.

Nor is this life-impulse (*élan de la vie*) produced in the void, or objectless. It rests upon a feeling inherent in every conscious individual, the feeling of dependence which every man experiences with respect to universal being. Which of us can escape this feeling of absolute dependence? Not only is our destiny, in principle, decided outside ourselves and apart from ourselves according to the general laws of cosmical evolution, in the course of which we appear at a given time and place with a heritage of forces which we have not chosen or produced, but, not being able to discover in ourselves or in any series of individuals the sufficient reason of our existence, we are obliged to seek outside ourselves, in universal being, the first cause and ultimate aim of our existence and our life. To be religious is, at first, to recognise, to accept with confidence, with simplicity and humility, this subjection of our individual consciousness; it is to bring this back and bind it to its eternal principle; it is to will to be in the order and the harmony of life. This feeling of our subordination thus furnishes the experimental and indestructible basis of the idea of God. This idea may possibly remain more or less indetermined, and may indeed never be perfected in our mind; but its object does not on that account elude our consciousness. Before all reflection, and before all rational determination, it is given to us and, as it were, imposed on us in the very fact of our absolute dependence; without fear we may establish this equation: the feeling of our dependence is that of the mysterious presence of God in us. Such is the deep source from which the idea of the divine springs up within us irresistibly. But it springs at once as religion and as an effect of religion.

At the same time, it is well to note at what a cost the mind of man accepts this subordination in relation to the principle of universal life. We have seen this mind in conflict with external things. The mind revolts against them because they are of a different nature to itself, and because it is the proud prerogative of mind to comprehend, to dominate, to rule things and not to be subordinate to them. Pascal's phrase is to the point: "Man is but a reed, the feeblest thing in nature; but he is a thinking reed. Were the universe to crush him, man would still be nobler than the universe that killed him, for he would be conscious of the calamity, and the universe would know nothing of the advantage it possessed." That is why the material universe is not the principle of sovereignty to which it is possible for man to submit. The superior dignity of spirit to the totality of things can only be preserved in our precarious individuality by an act of confidence and communion with the universal Spirit. It is only on a spiritual power that my consciousness does actually make both me and the universe to depend, and in making us both to depend on the same spiritual power, it reconciles us to each other, because, in that universal being conceived as spirit, both I and the universe have a common principle and a common aim. Descartes was right: the first step of the human mind desirous of confirming to itself the sense of its own worth and dignity is an essentially religious act. The circle of my mental life, which opens with the conflict of these two terms—consciousness of the ego, experience of the world—is completed by a third in which the other terms are harmonised: the sense of their common dependence upon God.

But is not this account of the genesis of religion too philosophic and too abstract to be capable of universal application? If it explains the persistence of the religious sentiment in epochs of high culture, can it also explain its appearance in the pre-historic ages of humanity? Those who raise this objection have not sufficiently marked the permanent nature of the initial contradiction which constitutes, at the beginning as at the end, the empirical life of man, and which renders it in all degrees so precarious and so miserable. It is not a contradiction created by logic. To experience it and to suffer from it man did not need to wait until he became a philosopher. It manifested itself in the terrors of the savage in presence of the cataclysms of nature, in the midst of the perils of the primeval forest not less than in our troubled thought in presence of the enigma of the universe and the mystery of death. The expression of human misery and the consciousness thereof are different things; the religious thrill which brings relief, at bottom is the same. Pascal, with all his knowledge, did not experience less distress than primitive man, when he exclaimed: "The eternal silence of the infinite spaces terrifies me." The disciple of Kant, shutting himself up in despair within the impassable limits of phenomenal knowledge, or the disciple of Schopenhauer ending in the internecine conflict between intellect and will, are they not smitten with a feeling of impotence still more painful, and, when they cease to reason in order to decide to live, do they not feel forming within themselves, and in spite of themselves, a sigh which is the beginning of a prayer?

Religion, therefore, is immortal. Far from drying up with time, the spring from whence it flows in the human soul enlarges, deepens, and becomes more rich under the twofold action of philosophic reflection and of the painful experiences of life. Those who predict its approaching end mistake for religion that which is only its outward and fleeting expression. The periodical crises in which it seems as if it must perish, renew its traditions and its forms, and, so far from proving its weakness, demonstrate its fecundity and its faculty of rejuvenescence. Never, in all history, has the human soul been seen entirely naked. On this tree, in which the sap divine mounts ever, the leaves of one season only fall, however dry they may be, under the pressure of new leaves. Religious beliefs do not die; they are simply transformed. Let the friends of religion then cease to be alarmed and its enemies to rejoice. The hopes of the one and the fears of the other show an equal misconception of that which is its essence and its principle. If they seek it in themselves, they will find it all the more living in their inner life, the more its traditional forms outside themselves seem menaced. The sigh, the impulse, or the melancholy of the soul in distress are more religious than an interested or mechanical devotion. There are hours when the heresy which suffers, and which seeks and prays, is much nearer the source of life than the intellectual obstinacy of an orthodoxy incapable, as it would seem, of comprehending the dogmas that it keeps embalmed. Let the men who despise religion learn first to know it; let them see it as it is—the inward happy crisis by which human life is transformed and an issue opened up to it towards the ideal life. All human development springs from it and ends in it. Art, morals, science itself fade and waste away if this supreme inspiration be wanting to them; the irreligious soul expires as if from lack of breath. Man is not; he has to make himself; and in order to this he must mount from the darkness and bondage of earth to light and liberty. It is by religion that humanity begins in him, and it is by religion that it is established and completed.

3. *Religion is the Prayer of the Heart*

We shall now be able to define the essence of religion. It is a commerce, a conscious and willed relation into which the soul in distress enters with the mysterious power on which it feels that it and its destiny depend. This commerce with God is realised by prayer. Prayer is religion in act—that is to say, real religion. It is prayer which distinguishes religious phenomena from all those which resemble them or lie near to them, from the moral sense, for instance, or aesthetic feeling. If religion is a practical need, the response to it can only be a practical action. No theory would suffice. Religion is nothing if it is not the vital act by which the whole spirit seeks to save itself by attaching itself to its principle. This act is prayer, by which I mean, not an empty utterance of words, not the repetition of certain sacred formulas, but the movement of the soul putting itself into personal relation and contact with the mysterious power whose presence it feels even before it is able to give it a name. Where this inward prayer is wanting there is no religion; on the other hand, wherever this prayer springs up in the soul and moves it, even in the absence of all form and doctrine clearly defined, there is true religion, living piety. From this point of view, perhaps a history of prayer would be the best history of the religious development of mankind. That history would be seen to commence in the crudest cry for help and to complete itself in perfect prayer which, on the lips of Christ, is simply submission to and confidence in the Father's will.

This concrete definition of religion has the advantage of correcting by completing that of Schleiermacher. It reconciles the two antithetic

elements which constitute the religious sentiment:
the passive and the active elements, the feeling of
dependence and the movement of liberty. Prayer,
springing up out of our state of misery and
oppression, delivers us from it. There is in it
both submission and faith. Submission makes us
recognise and accept our dependence, faith transforms that dependence into liberty. These two
elements correspond to the two poles of the
religious life; for in all true piety man prostrates
himself before the omnipotence that encompasses
him, and he rises with a feeling of deliverance
and of concord with his God. Schleiermacher
erred in insisting only upon resignation. Thenceforth he could neither escape Pantheism in order
to arrive at liberty, nor find any link between the
religious and the moral life. Religion, then, is a
free act as well as a feeling of dependence. And
such is the character and the virtue of the act of
prayer that everything is transformed by it. The
crushing feeling of my defeat becomes the joyful
and triumphant feeling of my victory. Each of
these states is changed into its opposite, so that
the truly religious man lives at once in a free
obedience and in an obedient liberty. If religion
has often been an oppressive power and an instrument of servitude, it has been at least as often the

mother of all the liberties. The force which bows me down is that which also lifts me up, for it passes into my soul. The God that I adore comes in the end to be an inward God whose presence drives away all fear and places me beyond the reach of all the menaces of things. The conscious realisation of this presence of God, —that is the true salvation of my being and my life.

I now understand why "natural religion" is not a religion. It deprives man of prayer; it leaves God and man at a distance from each other. No intimate commerce, no interior dialogue, no exchange between them, no action of God in man, no return of man to God. At bottom, this pretended religion is nothing but philosophy. It arises in periods of rationalism, of criticism, of impersonal reason, and has never been anything but an abstraction. The three dogmas in which it is summed up—the existence of God, the immortality of the soul, and the obligation of duty—are but the inorganic residue, the *caput mortuum*, found at the bottom of the crucible in which all positive religions are dissolved. This natural religion, so called, is not found in Nature; it is no more natural than it is religious. A lifeless, artificial creation, it shows hardly any of the characteristic marks of a religion. For the moment, it may seem to have the advantage of escaping the attacks of scientific criticism. On trial, it is found to be less resistant than any other. The self-same reason that constructed it destroys it, and its dogmas are perhaps more compromised to-day in face of modern thought than those it professes to replace.

Religion then is inward prayer and deliverance. It is inherent in man and could only be torn from his heart by separating man from himself, if I may so say, and destroying that which constitutes humanity in him. I am religious, I repeat, because I am a man, and neither have the wish nor the power to separate myself from my kind.

CHAPTER II

RELIGION AND REVELATION

1. *The Mystery of the Religious Life*

"THOU wouldst not seek me hadst thou not already found me." In this word that Pascal heard amid his restless search, the whole mystery of piety is disclosed. If religion is the prayer of man, it may be said that revelation is the response of God, but only on condition that we add that this response is always, in germ at least, in the prayer itself.

This thought struck me like a flash of light. It was the solution of a problem that had long appeared to me to be insoluble. I had never read without a certain amount of doubt, and as an oratorical exaggeration, that promise made by Jesus to His disciples with so strange an assurance: "Ask, and it shall be given you: seek, and ye shall find: knock, and it shall be opened unto you. For every one that asketh, receiveth: and he that seeketh findeth ; and to him that knocketh it shall be opened" (Matt. vii. 7, 8). Jesus had experienced a truth of which I am only beginning to catch sight: no prayer remains unanswered, because God to whom it is addressed is the One who has already inspired it. The search for God cannot be fruitless: for, the moment I set out to seek Him, He finds me and lays hold of me. Allow me to reflect a little longer on this mystery. I seem as if I were listening to these gospel words and promises for the first time. They sound in my ears like deep and solemn music which, bearing to me the echo of the religiously active soul of Jesus, brings succour to my own. The religious life, then, is not a fixed state: it is a movement of the soul, it is a desire, a need. The love of truth, is it not the principle of science? To love truth above all things, is not that in some way to be already in the truth? The point of departure, the inward beginning of a real righteousness, is not this repentance, that is to say the pain of not being righteous? I understand now why the Christ has made humility and confidence the sole conditions of entrance to His kingdom, why His Word has made riches spring from poverty, health from sickness, and satisfaction from the very intensity of need. Secret of the gospel, mysterious laws of spirit, pure moral essence of the kingdom of God, paradoxes which disconcert the man immersed in the ideas of the life of sense and self, but which contain the highest realities of moral life, reveal yourselves with ever-growing clearness to my consciousness, since, for me, on this first revelation all the rest depend!

I turn to another thought of Pascal. "Piety," he says, "is God sensible to the heart." If so, it is evident that in all piety there is some positive manifestation of God. The ideas of religion and revelation are therefore correlative and religiously inseparable. Religion is simply the subjective revelation of God in man, and revelation is religion objective in God. It is the relation of subject and object, of effect and cause, organically united; it is one and the same psychological phenomenon, which can neither subsist nor be produced save by their conjunction. It is as impossible to isolate as it is to confound them.

I conceive therefore that revelation is as universal as religion itself, that it descends as low, goes as far, ascends as high, and accompanies it always. No form of piety is empty; no religion is absolutely false; no prayer is vain. Once more, revelation is in prayer and progresses with prayer. From a revelation obtained in a first prayer is born a purer prayer, and from this a higher revelation. Thus light grows with life, truth with piety. This makes it possible for me to enter into communion and sympathy with all sincerely religious souls, however simple and however crude or gross their worship and their faith; but if I can comprehend them, I cannot always speak their language or share their ideas. All religions are not equally good, nor are all prayers acceptable to my consciousness. To return to exploded superstitions or to beliefs now recognised to be illusory is as much a moral impossibility as it would be for a full-grown man to return to the puerilities of his childhood. Revelation therefore is not a communication once for all of immutable doctrines which only need to be held fast. The object of the revelation of God can only be God Himself, and if a definition must be given of it, it may be said to consist of the creation, the purification, and the progressive clearness of the consciousness of God in man,—in the individual and in the race.

From this point of view, I see very clearly that the revelation of God never needs to be proved to any one. The attempt would be as contradictory as it is superfluous. Two things are equally impossible: for an irreligious man to discover a divine revelation in a faith he does not share, or for a truly pious man not to find one in the religion he has espoused and which lives in his heart. With what, moreover, and how could it be proved that light shines except by forcing those who are asleep to awake and open their eyes? All serious Apologetics must insist as a necessary starting-point on the awakening and conversion of the soul.

Having always been religious, mankind has never been destitute of revelation, that is to say of witness more or less obscure, more or less correctly interpreted, of the presence in it and the action of God. But if men have always maintained some relation and some commerce with the deity, they have not always represented in the same manner the mode in which communications have been received from Him. The notion of revelation has progressed with the growth of mental enlightenment and with the nature of the piety. It is therefore necessary to criticise that notion and to see what it has now become for us. It is to this examination that I shall devote this second meditation. The idea of revelation has passed through three phases in the course of history: the mythological, the dogmatic, and the critical.

2. *The Mythological Notion of Revelation*

Among the faculties of man, the first to awaken in the mental life of the child and of the savage is the imagination. All literatures begin with chants, all histories with legends, and all religions with myths or symbols. Poetry always makes its appearance before prose. One can only see the effect of an inveterate rationalism in the promptitude with which men are scandalised at any attempt to point out in the Bible or around the cradle of Christianity legends and myths serving as sacred vehicles for the purest and sublimest religious revelations, as if the divine Spirit, in order to be intelligible to the simple and the ignorant, could not as well avail Himself of the fictions of poetry as of logical reasonings, of the chants of the angels at Bethlehem as of the rabbinical exegesis and argumentations of the Apostle Paul. A myth is false in appearance only. When the heart was pure and sincere the veils of fable always allowed the face of truth to shine through. And why so much disdain? Does not childhood run on into maturity and old age? What are our most abstract ideas but primitive metaphors which have been worn and thinned by usage and reflection?

It is none the less true, as St. Paul says, that in advancing in age we have left behind the speech and thought of infancy. The first men did not know how to distinguish between the substance and the form of their beliefs. This distinction has become easy to us. The most conservative minds can no longer read the stories or the monuments of the ancient religions without criticising and translating them.

The men of other times, timid and ingenuous as children, saw everywhere material signs by which they believed the will of the gods was manifested. They early formed the art of divination—an essentially religious art. It is found among all peoples, the ancient Hebrews not excepted. The thunder was to them the voice of God. They consulted Him by the Urim and Thummim, and by the sacred ephod. They did not doubt, any more than the Greeks, either the divine origin or the prophetic sense of dreams. Elsewhere they evoked the dead, they interrogated the flight of birds, they listened to the sound of the wind in the foliage of the oaks, or to the noise of waters in sonorous caverns. That was an external and, in some sort, physical conception of revelation, from which modern peoples have escaped, but with which all set out.

In the oldest traditions of Hebraism, God speaks to Adam, to Noah, to Abraham, to Moses, as one man speaks to another, by articulate sounds perceived by the ear. The sacred formula, *Thus saith the Lord*, serves as the uniform introduction to civil, political, and ritual, as well as to moral and religious, laws. Religion then embraced and regulated all the life. The great empires of antiquity all claim a divine origin. As to ancient legislations, there is not one that is not said to have come from heaven. The Egyptians refer theirs to the god Thoth or Hermes; Minos, in Crete, is said to have received his laws from Jupiter; Lycurgus, in Sparta, from Apollo; Zoroaster, in Persia, from Ahura Mazda; Numa Pompilius, at Rome, from the nymph Egeria. Moses does not stand alone. I am not here comparing the value of the things; I am simply pointing out the identity of the representations.

Nor was it only religious and political institutions that they referred to the will of the gods; they referred to it all kinds of decisions and enterprises; declarations of war, raids to make, the order of battle, the extermination of the vanquished, the sharing of the spoils, conditions of peace, expiations to be made; everything was done in obedience to supernatural orders the authenticity of which no one thought of discussing. In the same way, a divine inspiration explained the gift of predicting the future, the eloquence of orators, the sagacity of statesmen, the genius of great soldiers, the verve of poets, and even the skill of the more famous artisans. "Legends"! it is said. No doubt. But these legends are universal. Men speak everywhere the same language, because everywhere they think in the same fashion.

A great progress, however, is accomplished in Israel. The notion of revelation gradually becomes interior and moral. Among the prophets, revelation is conceived of as the action of the Spirit of Jehovah entering and acting in the spirit of man. It is true that the mythical conception still persists and betrays itself in this: divine inspiration is represented as the invasion of a human being by another being alien to him,—as a sort of mental alienation or possession. The divine Spirit is represented as a force which comes from without, a wind from above which no one can resist, of which the elect are as much the victims as the organs. Its action is measured by the agitation and commotion of the inspired, by the disorder of their faculties, by the incoherence of their gestures and their speech. The delirium of man becomes the sign of the presence of God. Madmen, valetudinarians, epileptics, are regarded almost everywhere as the favourites of Heaven. Their strange words or acts men believe to be divine oracles delivered unconsciously and against the will.

This violent opposition between the supernatural action of the divine Spirit and the normal exercise of rational faculties is gradually attenuated in the course of the ages. It is easy to see that in the great prophets of Israel the formula *Thus saith the Lord*, while still frequent and still expressing the same subjective certitude of inspiration, has become a simple rhetorical form. God speaks henceforth to His people by their eloquence, by their faith, by their genius. "The Spirit of the Lord God is upon me," cries the second Isaiah; "because the Lord hath anointed me to preach good tidings to the meek," etc. (Is. lxi. 1-3).

This evolution appears to have been completed in the soul of Christ. Here inspiration ceases to be miraculous without ceasing to be supernatural. It is no longer produced by fits and starts or intermittently. An ancient gospel ("The Gospel of the Hebrews") admirably marks this change. At the moment of His baptism the Holy Spirit says to Jesus: *Mi fili, te exspectabam in omnibus prophetis, ut venires et requiescerem in te. Tu enim es requies mea.* (My Son, in all the prophets I awaited Thy coming in order that I might repose in Thee. Thou art indeed my rest.)

Being continuous, the inspiration becomes normal. The ancient conflict between the divine Spirit and the human vanishes. The immanent and constant action of the one manifests itself in the regular and fruitful action of the other. God lives and works in man, man lives and works in God. Religion and Nature, the voice divine and the voice of conscience, the subject and the object of revelation, penetrate each other and become one. The supreme revelation of God shines forth in the highest of all consciousnesses and the loveliest of human lives.

This progress, is it not admirable? Should it not strike the attention all the more inasmuch as, instead of being the effect of rational criticism, it is, in Christianity, exclusively the work of piety? This, become more profound, has conquered the ancient antithesis created by the ignorance of early times. Divesting itself more and more of foreign and inferior elements, the idea of revelation has been found to be more human as it has become more inward, more constant, more strictly moral and religious. Christ has not given us a critical theory of revelation; He has done what is better; He has given us revelation itself—a perfect and permanent revelation; He presents God and man to us so intimately united in all the acts and moments of His inner life, that they become inseparable. The Father acts in His Son, and the Son reveals the Father to all who wish to know Him.

Though he still retained many remnants of the ancient mythological notion (visions, dreams, ecstasies, delirium of tongues), the Apostle Paul seized with energy the distinguishing characteristic of the Christian revelation, and propounded the theory of it with a sacred boldness. That theory consists in the effusion and habitation of the Holy Spirit in the souls of Christians who, in their turn, become "children of God," and enjoy, by this Spirit, the same direct and permanent communion with the Father. This Spirit is no longer an alien guest or a perturbing force; He becomes in us a second nature. That is why the Christian is set free from all the old tutelages; he judges everything and is judged by nothing; he has his law within himself, so that from this inspiration springs his autonomy and his liberty.

But neither this spiritual piety nor the lofty

conception which flows from it could long be sustained. Preoccupied in founding its authority, and only being able to succeed in it by returning to the idea of an external revelation, the Catholic Church made it to consist chiefly in rules and dogmas, and, by this change, it naturally transformed the mythological notion of revelation into a dogmatic notion not essentially different.

3. *Dogmatic Notion*

"The Greeks," said Paul, "seek philosophy; the Jews demand miracles." From these two tendencies combined, from Greek rationalism and Hebrew supernaturalism, sprang the new notion that may be summed up and defined thus: a divine doctrine legitimated by divine signs or miracles.

These two elements of the theory are mutually dependent, and form an indivisible whole. Given to man in a supernatural way, the doctrine surpasses the reach of the human understanding; hence it must not be imposed upon the mind by its own evidence or examined by natural reason. The supernatural doctrine demands supernatural proof. This proof can only be found in the miracles which have accompanied the doctrine from its birth. Thus mysteries, incomprehensible in the order of reason, will necessarily be established by inexplicable events in the order of Nature.

The theory, in this way, becomes coherent, but it is not complete. A third term must be added. The divine doctrine must be embodied in a form which distinguishes it from all others, and placed under an authority that guarantees it. For Protestantism, the form and the authority of revelation is—the Bible; for Catholicism, it is the Bible sovereignly interpreted by the Church. The scholastic notion of revelation is now complete. The doctors teach us to distinguish three things in it: the object, which is dogma; the form, which is Scripture; and the proof or criterion, which is miracle. This construction appears to be compact in all its parts; in reality it is so fragile and so artificial that it crumbles at a touch.

To make of dogma, that is to say of an intellectual datum, the object of revelation is, in the first place, to eliminate from it its religious character by separating it from piety, and in the next place it is to place it in permanent and irreconcilable conflict with the reason, which is always progressing. In vain do they appear to deduce this scholastic theory from the Bible; it is simply an unfaithful translation of the Biblical notion. They tear up from the soil of the religious life the revelation of God in order to constitute it into a body of supernatural verities, subsisting by itself, to which they make it an obligation and a merit to adhere, silencing, if needs be, both the judgment and the conscience. Faith, which, in the Bible, was an act of confidence and consecration to God, becomes an intellectual adherence to an historical testimony or to a doctrinal formula. A mortal dualism starts up in religion. It is admitted that orthodoxy may exist apart from piety, that a man may obtain and possess the object of faith apart from the conditions that faith presupposes, and, at a push, serve divine truth while inwardly an unbeliever and a reprobate. Get rid of this illusion, frivolous and irreligious man! Whatever your authorities in earth or heaven, you are not in the truth, because you are not in piety. God has not spoken anything to you. To the prophets He has spoken, doubtless, and to Christ and the apostles and the saints; to you He still remains a stranger and unknown. His revelation has not been to you a light, for you are walking in darkness. You are like the Jews who built the tombs of the prophets and crowned their memory with empty honours. Had you been living in the time of the men of God, you would have been the first to stone them.

This idea of revelation is at bottom entirely pagan. In the region of authentic Christianity you cannot separate the revealing act of God from His redeeming and sanctifying action. God does not enlighten, on the contrary He blinds those whom He does not save or sanctify. Let us boldly conclude, therefore, against all traditional orthodoxies, that the object of the revelation of God could only be God Himself, that is to say the sense of His presence in us, awakening our soul to the life of righteousness and love. When the word of God does not give us life, it gives us nothing. It is true that that presence and that action of the divine Spirit in our hearts become in them a light whose rays illumine all the faculties of the soul. But do not hope to enjoy that light apart from the central sun from which it flows.

The scholastic notion is not only irreligious; it is anti-psychological. In entering the human understanding this supernatural knowledge introduces into it a hopeless dualism. The sacred sciences are set up alongside the profane sciences without its being possible to organise them together into a coherent and harmonious body, for they are not of the same nature, they do not proceed from the same method, they do not accept the same control. You have thus a sacred cosmogony and a profane cosmogony, a sacred history of the origins of man and a purely human history of his beginnings, and of his first adventures, a divine metaphysic and another purely rational. How to make them live together and unite them? If, by a subtle theology, you succeed in rationalising dogma, do you not see that you destroy it in its very essence? If you demonstrate that it is essentially irrational, do you not feel that you are instituting an endless warfare between the authority of dogma and the authority of reason? One remembers the generous attempt of mediæval scholasticism, taken up again by the Protestant theologians of the seventeenth century, and one has not forgotten its twice fatal issue. One would need to have no notion of the laws of human thought to be astonished at it. Nominalism in the fifteenth century and rationalism in the eighteenth were the two natural heirs of orthodoxy.

The intervention of miracle as a *criterion* or proof of doctrine does not remove the difficulties of the theory; it multiplies and aggravates them. In consequence of the lapse of time, the incertitude of the documents, and the demands of modern thought, miracle, which formerly established the truth of religion, has become much more difficult to demonstrate than religion itself. The relation between the two has been reversed. The foundation of the edifice has become more ruinous than the building. Examples? Consider, then, on the one hand, the Decalogue, and on the other the thunders and lightnings of Sinai. Peals of thunder may have served to convince the Hebrews that the law of Moses came from the Eternal; for they looked upon thunder as revealing the presence, in some sort material and local, of their God. But who does not see that it is much easier to-day to prove the excellence and the truth of the *Ten Words* of the Law than the divine character of the most terrible of tempests? Make the opposite experiment: you are familiar with the Books of Joshua, Judges, Kings. You have read in them those orders issued by Jehovah for the total extermination of peoples whose crime was the defence of their country against the invaders. Prodigies abound in them: the walls of Jericho fall down at the sound of trumpets, etc., etc. Are these events sufficient to warrant us in admitting the affirmation of the Hebrew historian that these terrible reprisals, these crimes and violences, which were then common in all the

Semitic tribes, were commanded either by the heavenly Father of Jesus Christ or by the impartial God of the universe? Our conscience resists and protests. Prodigies the most brilliant cannot make it do violence to itself or bend the law of righteousness and love beneath any manifestation, however striking, of brute force. Let us go further; let us come to the miracles of Christ. Let us interrogate the best Christians of our time: let us ask ourselves, Is it the cures that Jesus wrought which make us believe to-day in the divine truth of His word or which give authority to the Sermon on the Mount? Is it not rather the Gospel that helps us to believe in the miracles by persuading us that a man who spake like this man must have been able to do things and work works as beautiful and as wonderful as the words which He spoke? The most conservative Apologists of the traditional school confess to-day that miracle has lost its evidential force; it might move those who witnessed it, but its action and its prestige have necessarily been diminishing day by day for the generations which have followed them.

What if we were to press the idea of miracle itself which is in process of vanishing in proportion as the idea of Nature is transformed?

What is Nature? Who knows its secrets and its limits? The theory of the evolution of things and beings, does it not show Nature to us as in travail, and as if perpetually giving birth to marvels? And if this creative energy which is in it can only religiously be referred to the constant activity of God in the universe and in history, how can we still oppose the laws of Nature to the will of God? Moreover, nothing is to-day more indeterminate, more impossible to define than the notion of miracle; it floats without ever being able to fix itself, between the idea of an absolute violation of the laws of Nature now no longer witnessed anywhere, to that entirely relative one of an extraordinary event, which, seeing that it may be encountered everywhere, no longer proves anything.

Lastly, if from the *object* and the *criterion* of revelation, we pass to the *form* which conserves and warrants it, *i.e.* to the Bible, questions become still more numerous and insoluble. In the seventeenth century the notion of the Bible and that of revelation were coincident and commensurate. But this identity depended upon two dogmas much impaired to-day. The one was the divine origin of the two Biblical Canons, *i.e.* of the Old and New Testaments: the other, the verbal inspiration of all holy Scripture, considered as divinely dictated.

History and exegesis have dissipated the illusions and the ignorance on which these two strange affirmations rested. The Bible appears to us as the work, slowly and laboriously constructed, of the ancient Jewish Synagogue, and of the Early Christian Church. It needed more than four centuries to establish and to delimitate the New Testament. The books which compose it were still in the time of Eusebius divided into two classes: books admitted everywhere and books contested. Why then should we not have the same liberty as Origen of doubting the authenticity of 2 Peter, *e.g.*, or as Denis of Alexandria in discussing the apostolic origin of the Apocalypse? As to the theory of verbal inspiration, which makes the sacred writers God's penmen merely, no savant nowadays can defend it, so thoroughly have biblical studies set forth the personal originality of each of them, and the merits or the imperfections of their works. Moreover, the distinction clearly made in all the schools between the sacred writings and revelation must be considered as an inalienable conquest of modern theology. There is no one now who does not admit this truth, which would have seemed intolerable to our fathers, namely, that the word of God is in the Bible, but that all the Bible is not the word of God.

If this be so one sees new questions surging up and awaiting solution. What is the relation of the word of God to the Bible? By what sign may we recognise the first and distinguish the second? Further, if there be any word of God outside the Bible, if there has been any revelation of God beyond the limits of the Hebrew people and primitive Christianity—and how can we deny this without denying the worth of religion?—what relation is there to establish, and what synthesis to make, between the biblical revelation and the other revelations suited to the various human families? Lastly, what place does the religion of Jesus occupy in the religious evolution of humanity? Modern theology seems deaf to these questions. Despairing of a solution, it hesitates to approach them. But they must be answered. Contemporary philosophy presses them upon the conscience of Christians. The scholastic theory, it is clear, cannot bring any solution to these new problems. As soon as the distinction is made in our consciousness between the word of God and the letter of holy Scripture, the first becomes independent of all human form and of all external guarantee. It is with it as with the light of the sun. It is only recognised by the brightness with which it floods us. But take care: to introduce this criterion of religious and moral evidence into the scholastic theory is to deposit an explosive in the heart of it which shatters it to atoms. . . . I leave to others the task of masking or repairing the ruins. A task more urgent and more fruitful awaits us. We must build up, on a new principle, a new theory of revelation, a theory that will at once bear the test of criticism and give satisfaction to piety.

4. *Psychological Notion*

To return to psychology. In all piety there is some positive manifestation of God. Otherwise, one might question the value of religious phenomena.

Three consequences follow: the revelation of God will be evident, interior, progressive.

It will be interior, because God, not having phenomenal existence, can only reveal Himself to spirit, and in the piety that He Himself inspires.

If revealers and prophets believed they heard the voice of God outside themselves they were the victims of a psychological illusion that analysis discerns and dissipates. The old theologian was right who said:

Nulla fides si non primum Deus ipse loquitur; Nulla que verba Dei nisi quæ in penetralibus audit Ipsa fides.[1] This interior revelation is only made, it is true, in connection with some external event of Nature or of History. If wonder is the beginning of philosophy it is also the commencement of piety. Religious emotion does not spring up by chance and unconditionally. But external signs are only revealers for those who know how to comprehend them, and who are able to interpret them in a religious sense. That is why the distinction sometimes made between the *manifestation* of God in things and divine *inspiration* in consciousness, between the sign or external miracle and the inward word, is of little worth except for pedagogic purposes. The manifestation of God in Nature or in History is always a matter of faith. It would only appear to be such in the light on the hearth of consciousness. Put out that inner light and everything speedily becomes obscure: "If the light that is in thee be darkness, there will be darkness round about thee," says Jesus. To the deaf man the universe

[1] There is no faith save in the heart where God has first made Himself heard, and there are no divine words except those which faith hears in the inmost sanctuary of the soul.

is mute. The starry heavens which bent the pensive brows of Newton and of Kant before the majesty of God, said nothing to Laplace. Lit up within, the soul of Christ saw everywhere the signs of God. Caiaphas saw none. In the cross of Jesus, where St. Paul discerned the manifestation of the wisdom and the power of God, the Pharisees had only seen the crushing proof that this Messiah was a mere impostor.

This inward revelation will be also *evident*. The contrary would imply a contradiction. He who says revelation says the veil withdrawn, the light come. True, the word *mystery* is often on the lips of Jesus, and in the writings of the New Testament; but, when applied to the essence of the Gospel it never has the meaning which is given to it later in the language of theology. The mystery of which Jesus, Paul, and the Apostles speak is a revealed mystery, *i.e.* a mystery which has become evident to pure hearts and pious souls through the public preaching of it. The Gospel is not obscurity; it is daylight, and it is nonsense to demand a criterion of evangelical revelation other than itself, any other evidence, *i.e.*, than its own truth, beauty, and efficiency.

Lastly, this revelation will be *progressive*. It

will be developed with the progress of the moral and religious life which God begets and nourishes in the bosom of humanity. The word of God is not that of a poor human founder who formulates in abstract terms ideas which are but the pale shadows of things. It is essentially creative. It carries with it all the substance of being and all the potency of life. It realises that which it proclaims, and never manifests itself except by its works. When God wished to give the Decalogue to Israel, He did not write with His finger on tables of stone; He raised up Moses, and from the consciousness of Moses the Decalogue sprang. In order that we might have the Epistle to the Romans, there was no need to dictate it to the Apostle; God had only to create the powerful individuality of Saul of Tarsus, well knowing that when once the tree was made the fruit would follow in due course. The same with the Gospel; He did not drop it from the sky; He did not send it by an angel; He caused Jesus to be born from the very bosom of the human race, and Jesus gave us the Gospel that had blossomed in His inmost heart. Thus God reveals Himself in the great consciousnesses that His Spirit raises, fills, illumines one by one; they form a sacred theory through the ages and leave on history a track of light which brightens, broadens to the perfect day.

A new and graver problem here arises. This revelation, made in the depths of the human soul, remains individual and subjective. How will it become objective and concrete? How will it be made an educating, saving power? This problem would be insoluble if Leibniz was right, if human souls were independent monads, closed against and impenetrable to one another, if it had been necessary, in a word, to regard them as absolute entities, posited from the beginning by the Creator. But they are nothing of the kind. Social philosophy has sufficiently demonstrated that no individual exists either by himself or for himself alone. In each man it is humanity that is realised—that is to say, a moral life common to all. Moral goods are in essence universal. They do not exist, doubtless, apart from the consciousness of the individual; but no consciousness acquires them without acquiring them, in principle at least, for all others.

Whence comes that religious kinship of souls, that facility of communion between them, and that infinite extension and prolongation of one and the same inspiration, if not from the presence in each of the same indwelling God? Men are only divided by their external idols. In proportion as they plumb their being and descend into the depths of their spiritual nature, they discover the same altar, recite the same prayer, aspire to the same end. It is for this profound reason that individual revelations become universal. There are only prophets chosen of God because there is a general vocation and election of all men. If humanity were not potentially and in some degree an Immanuel (God with us), there would never have issued from its bosom Him who bore and revealed this blessed name. The religious experience He passed through, He passed through for us; the victory He won was for our advantage and is repeated indefinitely in every sincere soul that joins itself to Him to live His life. Thus the revelation of God given at one point and in one consciousness infallibly shines forth, perpetuates and multiplies itself. A vibration set up in a soul resounds in kindred souls. An illumined consciousness illuminates in turn. There are religious filiations, just as there are historical genealogies. Thus the inner revelation becomes consistent and objective in history; it forms a chain, a continuous tradition, and becoming incarnate in each human generation, remains not only the richest of heritages, but the most fecund of historical powers.

One step more. Let us follow this historical incarnation of religious tradition into its most material form. The inner experiences of men of God and the witness of them that they give to the world, express themselves naturally in speech, and this in its turn is transformed into Scripture. It is in this way that in all civilised religions divine revelation is presented to man in the form of a sacred writing; everywhere it is gathered into collections of sacred books which have been called the bibles of humanity. While all these have been born according to the same psychological and historical laws, it does not follow that they have all the same value, or that an unintelligent syncretism has the right to mix together the various elements in them to make of them one common and characterless Bible. No; each of them naturally belongs to a particular stage in the ladder of divine revelations, and there we must leave them. The highest will always be that which contains the deepest and purest expression of inward religion, and consequently offers to man the most precious treasure. The rank of the Hebrew and Christian Bible is thus found to be logically determined by the moral worth of the Hebrew and the Christian religions. But in leaving historical criticism and religious experience to make here the necessary demonstration and render it daily more evident, we must once more call to mind the always human conditions of these written collections, of those at the top as well as those at the bottom of the ladder, conditions which forbid us ever to identify the letter and the spirit, the divine inspiration and the particular form in which it has been clothed.

God, wishing to speak to us, has never chosen any but human organs. With whatever inspiration He has endowed them, that inspiration has always therefore passed through human subjectivity; it has only been able either to express or to translate itself in the language and the turn of mind of a particular individual and of a particular time. Now, no individual and historical form can be absolute. If the contents are divine, the vessel is always earthen. The organ of the revelation of God necessarily limits it. It must of necessity accommodate itself to the limits of human receptivity. How could it possibly enter and mingle with the changing waves of the intellectual and moral life of humanity unless it flowed in the bed of the river and between its banks?

However incontestable this historical complexity of the divine and human elements in religion, most men seem incapable of comprehending it, and of frankly accepting it. Men of little faith, we feel ourselves lost the moment men take from us the illusion that we ever have before us and outside of us the divine revelation in an objective and unadulterated form, when alongside authority and tradition they make a place for the freedom and the interpretation of consciousness. Is there then some chemistry by which we can separate that which God has joined so indissolubly? Has life ever been seen apart from living beings, or light apart from luminous vibrations? Why not make an effort to see that the wisdom of God is infinitely greater than our own, and that what He has given us is better than that of which we dreamed. Life and light, even if they are *not* absolute, propagate themselves with none the less force.

Lastly, what is the criterion by which you may recognise an authentic revelation of God in the books you read, in the things you are taught? Listen: only one criterion is sufficient and infallible: every divine revelation, every religious experience fit to nourish and sustain your soul, must be able to repeat and continue itself as an actual revelation and an individual experience in your own consciousness. What cannot enter thus as a permanent and constituent element into the woof of your inner life, to enrich, enfranchise, and transform it into a higher life, cannot be for you a light, or, consequently, a divine revelation. The spirit of life is not there. Do not believe that the prophets and founders have transmitted to you their experience in order to make yours needless, or that their revelation has been brought to you in a book for you to receive passively and as if it were an alien thing. Religious truth cannot be borrowed like money, or, rather, if you do so borrow it you are none the richer. Remember what the Samaritans said to the woman: "Now we believe, not because of thy saying: for we have heard Him ourselves, and know that this is indeed the Christ, the Saviour of the world" (John iv. 42). Thus the divine revelation which is not realised in us, and does not become immediate, does not exist for us. And I admire the counsel of God, Who, wishing to raise man into liberty, did not give to him an objective revelation which would have become to him a yoke of bondage. The aim of tradition is liberty, and liberty returns lovingly to tradition when, instead of finding it a yoke, it sees in it only a help, an aliment, a guide.

5. *Conclusion*

Such, in its principle, and with all its consequences, is the new idea of revelation given to us by psychology and history. Before it vanish the insoluble antitheses and conflicts raised by scholasticism between supernatural and natural revelation, between what the theologians call immediate and mediate, between a universal and a special revelation. Synthesis is made, and peace is re-established.

There is not and could never have been two revelations different in nature and opposed to each other. Revelation is one, in different forms and various degrees. It is at once supernatural and natural: supernatural by the cause which engenders it in souls, and which, always remaining invisible and transcendent, never exhausts or imprisons itself in the phenomena it produces; natural, by its effects, because, realising itself in history, it always appears therein conditioned by the historical environment and by the common laws which regulate the human mind.

This revelation also is immediate for all, for the least in the kingdom of heaven, as for the greatest of the prophets; for God desires to admit them all into direct and personal communion with

Himself; and it is equally mediate for all; for it comes to none, whether prophets or their disciples, unconditionally, and without previous preparation.

Lastly, it is not less false and futile to oppose universal revelation to particular revelations as two exclusive quantities. Particular revelations enter into general revelation as varieties into species. Every special revelation, if it be really from God, is human, and tends to become universal; every general revelation was once individual, for it could only have been made in an individuality. Among the men and peoples chosen by God as organs there is inequality in gifts but solidarity in the common work. We must not mistake the one or the other. The religious vocation of humanity does not exclude—it prepares and supports—the particular vocation of Israel. In this national vocation there is a place for that of the prophets, and, among the prophets, for the vocation of Him who was their heir, and in Whom the revelation of God was completed, because in His consciousness was realised perfectly the very idea of piety.

Is everything explained in religion, then, and nothing left obscure? Far from that! There remains the ground from which emerges the conscious and moral life of the soul; there remains that initial mystery, the relation in our consciousness between the individual and the universal element, between the finite and the infinite, between God and man. How can we comprehend their co-existence and their union, and yet how can we doubt it? Where is the thoughtful man to-day who has not broken the thin crust of his daily life, and caught a glimpse of those profound and obscure waters on which floats our consciousness? Who has not felt within himself a veiled presence and a force much greater than his own? What worker in a lofty cause has not perceived within his own personal activity, and saluted with a feeling of veneration, the mysterious activity of a universal and eternal power? *In Deo vivimus, movemur et sumus.* There is perhaps no other mystery in religion; at all events all others are but particular forms of this. But this mystery cannot be dissipated, for, without it, religion itself would no longer exist.

CHAPTER III

MIRACLE AND INSPIRATION

IN speaking of revelation we have already touched on the doctrines of inspiration and of miracle, which are dependencies of it, and, as it were, constituent parts. But these two notions are still so obscure in the public mind, and give rise to so many and such lively controversies, that it may be well to return to them and study them by themselves and in some detail.

In this matter there are two causes of dispute and misunderstanding. The first is that everybody believes he ought to begin by giving his own personal and arbitrary definition of miracle, and afterwards explain by way of deduction why he believes or does not believe in it. The debate thus turns on a question of terminology—that is to say, on a vain and barren logomachy. The second cause is that the defenders of miracle always keep to abstractions, instead of following their contradictors on to the ground of criticism of miraculous stories and placing themselves in presence of the facts which alone make up the matter of the discussion. They believe they have gained everything when they have proved that God, according to the very definition of the idea that we have of Him, can do everything—which no one denies—while the problem consists not in knowing what God can do *in abstracto*, but what He has done *in concreto*, in Nature and in History. Now, in order to know what is really done, and whether there are or ever have been produced phenomena which must be referred to the immediate intervention, and to a particular volition of God, independently of the concurrence of second causes, this is evidently something that only the critical observation of facts, past or present, can teach us. Every other method of research and discussion is illusory.

Faithful to our own, we here place ourselves at the historical point of view. Convinced that ideas have a history, and are most clearly and surely defined by their very evolution, we shall confine ourselves to following and describing that evolution. We shall seek in the first place to ascertain the notion of miracle that was current in antiquity; after that we shall see what became of it in mediæval theology; and lastly we shall see into what elements it has resolved itself in modern times, as much at the point of view of science as of piety. As religious inspiration, properly speaking, is but a particular miracle, a miracle of the psychological order, the solution available for the one will apply to the other.

1. *The Notion of Miracle in Antiquity*

The primitive conception of Nature was animistic. In everything *astonishing*, extraordinary, men used to see the action of spirits like themselves, with whom their religious imagination peopled the heavens, the earth, the seas. They lived in miracle. It would be easier to enumerate the things that were not than the things that were to them miraculous. The word Nature, which has become so familiar and so indispensable to designate the regular course of things, does not exist in primitive languages. One does not meet with it even in the language of the Old Testament. This is because the conception it represents only came into existence later, and by a slow and laborious process, in the philosophy of the Greeks. The cosmos, ordered and harmonious and fixed, is the sublime creation of Hellenic reason. Elsewhere, no doubt, with experience of life and the daily return of phenomena, a certain order, the effect of custom, would exist around man and be established in his mind. He learned to distinguish between the habitual course of things and the prodigies which caused him wonder, fear, or hope, and in which he always saw the effect either of the favour or the anger of a demon or a god. His imagination, to which his ignorance gave free play, and his credulity, which religious terror held open to all impressions, stories, legends, wrapped his life in an atmosphere of marvel, gentle or terrible, but incessant. Eclipses, earthquakes, thunder, lightning, rainbows, deluges, accidents, maladies, etc.—these were the work of particular actors, personal, impassioned like man, hidden behind the scenes. Add to this the inventions of sorcerers and priests; . . . transport yourself into this first effervescence of the human faculties, into this luxuriant vegetation of poetical creation in the early human mind, and you will have some idea of what, for centuries on centuries, must have been the mental state of primitive historic humanity. Such, however, is the comparative poverty of human conceptions, that, when you come to catalogue these marvels, you see them reduced to a small number of miracles which turn up everywhere and again and again among all peoples. Their similarity approaches to monotony. ... The question for the moment is not whether these miraculous facts are real or not, but how the men who have transmitted them to us represented them. There is no doubt on this point. To them they were not simply astonishing facts that admitted of a natural explanation. Modern theologians and savants who seek and find for them explanations of this kind do not perceive that they contradict themselves, and that to explain miracle in this way is to destroy it. No; that which is miraculous in these events—to the contemporaries of Tarquin in Rome, of Joshua in Palestine, to the people in our own day—is this, that they are produced, contrary to the natural course of things, solely by a special intervention of the divine will. That is the mark and characteristic of ancient miracle. Efface it, for any reason whatever, and miracle disappears. That which makes it possible is ignorance of Nature and its laws: that which supports it is the religious belief in the existence of these supernatural wills and in their unexpected invasion of the succession of accustomed things. "Without this belief," as M. Ménégoz remarks,[1] "the birth of a myth or of a legend could not be explained.

---

[1] *La notion biblique du miracle* (Leçon d'ouverture), 1894.

St. Denis, decapitated, would not have been able to carry his head." In fact, the miracles you find in the apocryphal legends are exactly of the same nature as those which are met with in narratives held to be more historical.

I must add that this notion of miracle is absolutely the same in Biblical as in profane literature. In a general way, no doubt, the supernatural in the history of Israel and in the early days of Christianity is of a more sober, more profoundly moral and religious character than it is everywhere else. But the sacred writers do not represent miracles differently. Without exception, they also conceive of them as a violation, by a particular volition of God, of the ordinary course of things. . . . Still, so far from being more striking or more numerous, miracles and prodigies in the Bible are rarer than elsewhere, clearer, less fantastic, more under law to conscience and to common sense. The worship of one God, invisible, spiritual, in whom centres the ideal of wisdom, reason, righteousness, conceived by the prophets, joined to the lack of imagination in the Hebrew race, has freed the Bible from the luxuriant growths of oriental mythologies and theogonies, as of the marvellous in the poesy of Greece. Nothing purifies the mind like a great moral idea around which all the rest organises itself. It is very remarkable that the great prophets, Isaiah, Amos, Micah, Jeremiah, John the Baptist, work hardly any miracles. If prodigy has penetrated into the life of Jesus at two or three points, the explanation is to be found in the mistakes or the legendary corruptions for which His biographers are alone responsible, and which criticism may eliminate without violence. Prodigy, properly so called, is quite foreign to the wholly moral conduct of His life, and to the strictly religious conception of His work. He did not found His religion on miracle, but on the light, the consolation, the pardon and the joy which His gospel, issuing from His holy, loving heart, brought to broken and repentant souls. His works proceeded only from His charity. Far from wishing to impose belief in His miracles, He often forbids men to divulge them. It is to the faith of the afflicted that He refers their cure. He turns away from the seductive invitations of miraculous *Messianism* as from the distrust or the curiosity of an incredulous wisdom. To those who demanded of Him an indubitable prodigy come from heaven, He answers that no sign shall be given them save the preaching of repentance by the prophet Jonah. The whole temptation in the wilderness is simply a victory of the moral consciousness over the religion of physical prodigy. His filial piety to the Father raised Him above miracle itself and above the dualism that miracle supposes in Nature and in the divine action. He discovers in everything the signs of the presence, the will, the affection, of His Father. He accepts them, submits to them, celebrates them, without preoccupying Himself with the ordinary or the extraordinary manner in which they may be manifested. This absolute piety, absolutely pure and confident, succeeds in realising the unity of the world and the universal and continuous action of God, quite as well as the dialectic of a Scotus Eriginus or a Spinoza or a Hegel; for it suppresses still more radically the old and mortal antithesis of the natural and the supernatural. Nature in its expansion and its evolution—what is it but the very expression of the Will of the Father? How can you imagine then that there could ever be conflict in it between the order which reigns in it and the action of Him by whom that order is maintained day by day and moment by moment?

If the thought of Jesus was bounded by the ancient notion of miracle, it must be acknowledged that His piety was not imprisoned in it, but went beyond it. Not having come into the world to teach science, He contented Himself with the opinions He had inherited with the rest of His people, and which constituted the science of Nature of His little popular environment, without concerning Himself as to whether these opinions were erroneous or correct. Miracle was not then something essentially religious as it is to-day. Belief in miracles was not a sign of piety. Everybody shared in it, men of the world as well as men of God. Herod believed in them not less than the apostles. The Pharisees did not doubt them; they only denied the miracles of Jesus; they attributed them to Beelzebub. Christ did not doubt any more than they did that Satan and the demons wrought as many and perhaps more miracles than the messengers of God. He did not wish them to believe the doctrine because of the prodigy, but in the prodigy because of the doctrine. It will be seen how far they were at that time from the dualism of our day, and from the conflict created by scholasticism between science and piety.

When we examine this ancient notion of miracle, especially in the superior expression it receives in the Bible, we discover in it two things: it is made up of two judgments of a very different order: of an intellectual and scientific order, disclosing that which then existed in point of fact, a *naïf* and perfect ignorance of the nature and the laws of things; and of a judgment of a religious order, implying an absolute confidence in an all-good God who is almighty to respond to the cry of His children and to deliver them. These two judgments are so thoroughly blended in the biblical notion of miracle that orthodox theologians and irreligious philosophers agree in declaring them to be inseparable, and they would compel us to choose between a piety hostile to the elementary results of science, and a science radically hostile to piety. The dilemma is specious but false. To see it vanish it is only necessary to perceive that these two judgments, not being of the same nature, cannot be eternally *solidaire*. The settlement of the controversy in which Christian thought has been engaged for the last three centuries will consist in separating them.

. . . . .

2. *The Notion of Miracle in the Face of Modern Science and of Piety*

Modern science neither affirms nor denies miracle; it ignores it, necessarily. It is, for it, as if it did not exist.

Religious persons, who often look towards

science to ascertain what their faith may hope or fear from it, only consider its results, and as these are never definitive, but always variable, always being revised, enlarged, enriched, they secretly indulge the hope that a moment may come when science, which has not yet welcomed miracle, will welcome it; that such a fact, supported by such and such testimony, will in the end conquer its resistances and obtain a place in the category or the catalogue of scientific facts. They would quickly lose this illusion, if, turning away from the net results of science, they would fix their attention on its processes and methods of investigation. What is it, according to science, to know a phenomenon? It is to place it in a necessary link of succession, concomitance, and causality with other phenomena which explain it by analogy. Suppose a mysterious phenomenon without analogy and connection with any other; savants brought into its presence will declare themselves simply in a state of ignorance with respect to it. They will say they have not discovered the cause of it, that they cannot explain it; they will study it on every side a thousand times if necessary until they have torn out the heart of the mystery. Either they will succeed, or on this point there will never be science made or explanation established.

Savants, it is true, are the first to recognise and to proclaim, in all domains, the limitations of their knowledge. The most advanced are the most modest. They all have the feeling that their discoveries are but a beginning, and that the part of Nature they have explored is as nothing to that of which they are ignorant. They hold themselves in readiness to modify the laws they have established, to enlarge their hypotheses, to make new ones, to record all facts which observation may supply. That many facts astonish them and disconcert them, we see every day. But mark the attitude of the true savant in face of these new phenomena. Does he doubt a single moment that they obey laws, unknown perhaps, but certain? . . . There can only be science of that which is general and constant.

It is therefore absolutely chimerical to expect of science the establishment of any miracle whatever. . . . Miracle, according to the only tenable definition, and this is the ancient and traditional one, is a positive intervention of God in the phenomenal order and at a particular point. Now science knows only second causes. How could it ever seize in the course of these causes the immediate action of the First Cause? Is God a phenomenon that the eye of man can ever perceive in any phenomenal series? And is not this the reason why science despairs of ever proving scientifically the existence of God? It recognises itself to be impotent to step out of the relative, to resolve anything outside space and time, and it has removed from its domain all questions as to origin and aim, because it has no means of reaching them.

To perceive God and the action of God in the human soul and in the course of things is the business of the pious heart (Matt. v. 8). The affirmation of piety is essentially different from scientific explanation. It places us in the subjective and moral order of life, which no more depends on the order of science than the scientific order depends on piety. There cannot be conflict between these two orders, because they move on different planes and never meet. Science, which knows its limits, cannot forbid the act of confidence and adoration of piety. Piety, in its turn, conscious of its proper nature, will not encroach on science; its affirmations can neither enrich, impoverish, nor embarrass science, for they bear on different points and answer different ends. My child is ill; I procure for it the best advice and the best remedies; but confiding in God's mercy, I beg of Him to spare me my child, or, in any case, to help me to accept His will. The child recovers. What savant will forbid me to thank my heavenly Father? Will this be because my thanksgiving will be a denial of the science of the physician? Certainly not, for my gratitude will include the fact of the doctor, the medicine, the care bestowed, the whole series of second causes that have contributed to the recovery of my child. Was not this the piety of Jesus when He taught us to pray: "Our Father which art in Heaven: Thy will be done: Give us our daily bread"? Was He ignorant of the fact that in order to have bread we must sow wheat? No; but none the less He asked His food from God, because He knew also that, in the last resort, it is the will of God that makes the substance and the order of things, that it is He who clothes the lilies of the field, feeds the fowls of the air, makes His sun to shine upon the evil and the good, and sends upon the labourer's soil the early and the latter rain.

Reduced to its religious and moral significance, miracle, for Jesus, was the answer to prayer, as M. Ménégoz (*op. cit.* pp. 19-29) has clearly shown, and this altogether apart from the phenomenal mode in which the answer was produced. God only manifests Himself in extraordinary events in order that we may learn to recognise Him in ordinary ones. The child asks, the father grants; but the child does not trouble himself about the means by which his wishes are gratified. The pious man adores the ways he cannot comprehend. This confidence in the love and justice of God may be accompanied in the mind of the apostles and of Jesus Himself by imperfect or erroneous scientific ideas as to the mode of divine action in Nature. But it is not *solidaire*, with them, and may easily be detached in order to bring it into harmony with the views of our present science, as in the mind of Jesus and the apostles it was in harmony with the science of their time. For piety, the laws of Nature which have since then been revealed to us in their sovereign constancy, become the immediate expression of the will of God. The Christian submits to them instinctively, saying: "Thy will be done." Which is only saying that these laws, which are sometimes spoken of with a sort of horror, as of a blind and brutal fate, become religious and are consecrated in the eyes of piety by a divine authority. Why then should not piety offer to science and its revelations of Nature the same frank and joyous welcome as that accorded to them by scientists themselves? The opposition established by scholasticism between faith and science, is it not as irreligious as it is irrational, and has it not been one of the chief causes of the death of theology in the Church and of the triumph of incredulity in the present age?

While developing themselves on parallel lines, can science and faith remain isolated? Man is one, and his scientific activity, like his religious activity, tends to a synthesis. The synthesis will be found in a teleological consideration of the universe. This universal teleology, faith predicts it, science labours to realise it. It can only be established by this twofold concurrence. Without faith, knowledge of the universe is impossible; without phenomenal science all interpretation of the universe becomes illusory. Faith, therefore, must become more and more an act of confidence in God, and the scientific study of phenomena ever more profound and rigorous. Of course the teleological synthesis will never be completed here below, but it will always find a provisional and satisfying conclusion in the act of confidence and adoration towards God.

Science is perpetually becoming. If at times it closes to piety dear and familiar prospects, it necessarily and constantly opens new ones. If it takes away its crutches, it gives it wings. The contemplation of the harmony of the worlds which moves us religiously is, it seems to me, worth more to modern thought than the fatidical oracle, or the cry of the crow that frightened the good old woman of Rome. The more science progresses the more it puts into things the order and harmony of thought. It can only create a Cosmos more and more intelligible and, consequently, susceptible of an increasingly religious interpretation.

At the same time as science instituted its severest methods, it radically transformed its primary notion of Nature. This was conceived by the Cartesian Rationalism as a finished and coherent whole, a system of identical movements and phenomena which were produced by virtue of the same springs acting in the same circle (the vortices of Descartes). The familiar image under which they loved to represent it was that of a watch, constructed and wound up by the divine artificer once for all. Now, we see this dogma of the immutability of Nature going to join the other dogmas of the past. The theory of the ascensional evolution of beings, which renders miracle useless, shows Nature to us in the course of constant transformation and perpetual travail. Nothing in it is stable or final. Everything is preparatory to something else; each form of life is the preface to a higher form. What then is the hidden mystery which ferments in the bosom of this painful nature and endeavours to expand?

"The more cannot issue from the less," said the schoolmen, and no doubt in abstract logic they were right. But reality smiles at logic. It shows us everywhere the triumph of the opposite maxim. Perfection is at the beginning of nothing. Cosmic evolution proceeds always from that which is poorer to that which is richer, from the simple to the complex, from the homogeneous to the heterogeneous, from dead matter to living matter, from physical to mental life. At each stage Nature surpasses itself by a mysterious creation that resembles a true miracle in relation to an inferior stage. What then shall we conclude from these observations except that in Nature there is a hidden force, an incommensurable "potential energy," an ever open, never exhausted fount of apparitions at once magnificent and unexpected? How can such a universe escape the teleological interpretation of religious faith? For the moment, science may accord nothing more to piety; but piety has no need to ask more from it; for it has already in this way found safeguarded the three things which the old notion of miracle guaranteed to it: the real and active presence of God, the answer to prayer, and liberty to hope.

* * * * * *

3. *Religious Inspiration*

Passing by the subject of prophecy, which is a species of miracle, and admits of the same kind of explanation, it may be well to touch upon the subject of prophetic inspiration. The ancients represent it as a veritable state of possession. The spirit of the god or demon violently entered into the body of a man or woman, sometimes of an animal, and made of it an organ the more faithful in proportion as it was unconscious. Everybody knows the description given by Virgil of the Cumaean sybil at the moment of vaticination: " The god, the god, she cried," etc. (Aeneid VI. v. 45 et 77.)[1] It was a sort of frenzy or sacred delirium in which divine words involuntarily and sometimes unconsciously proceeded from the mouth of the possessed. Madmen, epileptics, idiots, hysterical persons, were regarded almost everywhere as sacred beings, friends and confidants of superior spirits. Their strange malady only

---

[1] Cf. Plato, *Meno. Timaeus*, 45.—Cicero, *De Divin.* 1. 2. 18. 31. Aristotle, *Problem.* xxx. p. 474.

seems explicable by the presence in them of one of these spirits.

The same ideas were current among the Hebrews, and are to be found both in the Old and in the New Testament. The prophets of Ramah, disciples of Samuel, and Saul himself, putting themselves by contagion into a state of delirium and "prophecy," are in a physical and mental state identical with that of the sybil of Cumae. The demons in possession of the man who was healed by Jesus were the first to divine and to salute His messianic dignity. The poor woman whom Paul healed at Philippi was haunted by "a spirit, a Python." The speakers with tongues at Corinth were thought by those present to be mad, and those at Jerusalem on the day of Pentecost looked like drunken men (1 Sam. x. 5-7 : Mark i. 24 : Acts xvi. 16-20 : 1 Cor. xiv : Acts ii. 13).

All these manifestations, formerly held to be supernatural, are now recognised as morbid phenomena, of which mental pathology describes the physiological causes, the natural course, the fatal issue. Even in frightful disorders order has been discovered; laws and remedies have been found for many of these sad afflictions. Formerly they deified these demented and tormented souls; in the Middle Ages, and up to the eighteenth century, they burned them; we pity them and care for them. This is much the best for all concerned.

Preoccupied with guaranteeing the infallibility of the sacred writings, the theology of the Fathers, of the scholastic doctors, and of the Protestant doctors of the seventeenth century, drew from this ancient notion of religious inspiration a dogmatic theory applicable to the divine oracles contained in the Bible. It seemed to them that the more passive the personal spirit of the writers was, the purer would be the word of God that they were charged to deliver when it reached us. At this point of view, the most faithful organ of God, the one that ought to inspire us with the greatest confidence, would be Balaam's ass. "The writer might be stupid," exclaims Gaussen, "but that which came from his hands would always be the Bible." Some have gone further by way of inventing images borrowed from the material order, such as, "the strings of a lyre," sounding beneath the divine bow, "the quills or pens of the Holy Spirit," etc., etc. The theory is familiar. It was developed throughout the Middle Ages until they came to say that God was the author and is alone responsible for the Bible, and for everything that is found in it; not only for the things and thoughts, but also for the words and style; not only for each word, but also for the vowels and the consonants. It only remained that they should have added the punctuation, not the least important matter in a connected discourse. Unhappily, the punctuation is absent from the oldest manuscripts.

Let us remind ourselves, however, that St. Paul, and Jesus Christ before him, had deposited the germ of a conception of religious inspiration more human, more psychological, and, at the same time, more real. Paul, who had ecstasies, visions, "tongues," always spoke of these doubtful privileges with a certain modesty, and that only when he was constrained to it, as if he had the feeling that there was something abnormal and morbid in these phenomena. On the other hand, he opposes to them a theory of true Christian prophecy conceived as a forcible, eloquent, irresistible proclamation of the mercy and justice of God; prophecy on the lips of the apostle, the poet, or the orator, springing from the assurance given him by the inward witness of the Holy Spirit that he is in perfect harmony with the divine thought. The force of this inspired prophecy comes from the luminous evidence which springs up within, which warms and kindles up the spirit like an inward fire. Under the influence of this illumination the apostle feels his strength increase tenfold; he rises at a mighty bound above himself. His faculties are carried to their maximum of energy and power. So far from being an inert, passive instrument, his intellect has never been intenser, richer; his thoughts more clear and more coherent; his words more fluent, more abundant, more pictorial and expressive; his voice more firm and resonant; his gestures more imperious. It is the hour when he is most himself, when his particular genius has freest play, when his moral originality is greatest, when he is most certainly the organ of eternal truth. Thus understood, religious inspiration does not differ psychologically from poetic inspiration. It presents the same mystery, but it is not more miraculous. It is not produced like a trouble violently introduced into the psychical life from without, but as a really fruitful force, acting from within, in harmony with all the laws and forces of the mind.

Does not experience establish and piety confirm this? When does an Amos, an Isaiah, a Jeremiah, a St. Paul, or a St. John, appear to us as the most authentic bearer of the word of truth and life, but in their most eloquent pages, where their personal genius, their faith, their thought, shine forth most freely? Religious inspiration is simply the organic penetration of man by God; but, I repeat, by an interior and indwelling God, and in such wise that when that penetration is complete, the man finds himself to be more really and fully himself than ever. It is with this mysterious action of the Spirit in the bosom of humanity as it is with the solar heat upon the plants that spring up from the soil. In regions where the heat is greatest and the other conditions favourable, plants which elsewhere are stunted attain their richest development and their greatest fecundity.

The inner root of this inspiration is only found in the piety common to religious men. It differs from it not in nature, but simply in intensity and energy. Prophetic inspiration is piety raised to the second power. There is no other mystery in it than the religious mystery *par excellence*. That is why this inspiration is essential to and promotes effectually the progress of the moral and religious life. They advance together through the ages as we now shall see.

CHAPTER IV

THE RELIGIOUS DEVELOPMENT OF HUMANITY

1. *The Social Element in Religion*

RELIGION is not merely a phenomenon of the individual and inner life: it is also a social and historical phenomenon. Psychology lays bare its root, but history alone reveals its power and range.

This social action of religion springs from its very essence. The phrase "communion of souls" is of religious origin and hue. The thing expressed by it—one of the most wonderful phenomena of collective moral life—is never perfectly realised save in religion and by religion. An identic faith, a common act of adoration, not merely brings souls together: it makes them live in each other, blends them into one soul in which each of them finds itself, multiplied, as it were, by all the rest. That is what is properly called "edification," by which I mean that feeling of joy, of force, of fulness of life, produced by the common act of worship in those who sincerely take part in it. That is the reason why men of the same religion have no more imperious need than that of praying and worshipping together. State police have always failed to confine growing religious sects within the sanctuary or the home. Their members have never been resigned to this comparatively solitary life; they have braved all interdicts and persecutions in order to turn it into social life and fraternal communion.

God, it is said, is the place where spirits blend. In rising towards Him man of necessity passes beyond the limits of his own individuality. He feels instinctively that the principle of his being is also the principle of the life of his brethren; that that which gives him safety must give it to all. In the same Religion, souls the most diverse, being affected in the same manner, become related to each other, and form a real family, united by closer, stronger bonds than those of blood. The religious life is a higher region. Those who rise into it feel the barriers fall which hemmed in their existence. They become free; they penetrate the souls of their neighbours and feel themselves to be penetrated by them; and all live one life, which, although it be larger and almost universal, is none the less very personal and very intense.

Have you ever been present in a crowd excited and exalted by religious enthusiasm? Have you felt the contagion? Then you can never forget it. It is said the early Christians were of one heart and one soul. Their community of faith, of hope, of love, went so far as to make them forget the idea of property and put their goods in common. In how many monastic orders or mystic sects has not this same need of equality and unity gone to the point of identity in costume and deportment, and even of the loss of name and personal individuality?

It is not surprising therefore that religion, capable of creating in modern times those moral societies called "Churches," should, in all ages, have been the strongest bond of natural societies, primitive families, savage tribes, great empires, civilised peoples. The first stone of every hearth was a sacred stone. The first tombstone was a monument of piety, and burial is an essentially religious ceremony. Before they were regarded as protectors without, tribal gods were the internal bonds of the tribe itself. All the individuals of the tribe saw in the god a father and an ever present head, so that religion came to double by this moral kinship their blood relationship. In this matter the great civilisations do not differ from the rest. All have a religious soul that differentiates and explains them. It is not merely morals and philosophy that are affected by religion, but literature, art, politics, social economy, and in a general way the whole destiny of men. The secret of a race is hidden in its religion. It is there that the forces of life and resistance to the causes of dissolution are concentrated. . . . Let us enter with deep piety therefore on the history of religion on the earth. . . . That history is still in embryo. The comparative study of religions has arisen within our time; it is still at its beginnings. . . . The idea of religious progress is a great and luminous idea, but it is not possible to apply it to all the details of history. Progress has not taken place along a single or continuous line. . . . On four or five points the progress is undeniable; it must suffice to point them out and mark their direction in order that we may foresee the supreme end to which this faltering and laborious march is tending.

In religions there are differences of degree and differences of kind: the one mark in the scale of evolution the successive movements of the religious consciousness in time; the others express the diversity and simultaneity of religions in space. The first are explained by inequalities of moral development; the second by variety of races, climates, civilisations. Take, for example, the Hebrew tradition; follow it in broad outline, and you will note religious forms which give birth one to another and constitute an historical development—the religion of the ancient Beni-Israel, prophetism, rabbinical pharisaism, Christianity, Mohammedanism: there, in a continuous evolution, you have what may be called differences of degree. But, on the other hand, consider the Mongolian or Chinese religions, those of ancient Mexico, of India, Egypt, or Greece: you have differences of kind which you cannot classify in a single scale. And, as some of these peoples have disappeared, and others been arrested in their growth, and as they have never marched abreast, it is impossible to compare them or to put into one category the religious forms which their history presents. But some attempt must be made to trace them out.

2. *Progress in the Outward Forms of Religion*

In this universal religious evolution the progress that is most apparent because most outward is the enlargement of the form of religion itself, the movement, often interrupted but never stopped, from the narrowest particularism to the most human universalism. . . . It is characteristic of all religion to propagate itself: that is the implicit affirmation that it is made for all men. Even when it is abased to the level of a recipe and of a magical secret that is hidden with a jealous selfishness, or even from a ferocious patriotism, there is the avowal that it might be serviceable to others. . . . But we must see how this passage from the particular to the universal is effected.

The beginnings of religion are everywhere the same. The number of cults at first is almost endless, but they vary very little from each other. It is impossible to write the history of barbarous religions, and it is useless to enumerate them. Nothing is more monotonous than the descriptions that have been attempted of them. Their most characteristic feature is, that at first they are confined to the family. Religion at this stage is a matter of instinct, and instinctive matters are always uniform. In mental life, diversity only appears with reflection and consciousness.

To the domestic and tribal succeeds the national stage of religion. Political federations are formed, and the religious as well as the social consciousness of the people is enlarged. This phenomenon is seen in Greece in its most interesting form. The religion of Greece, as witness the Homeric poems, was a confederation of local cults and deities, just as Hellas was a federation of previously unconnected tribes.

The conquests of Alexander and the extension of the Roman Empire greatly enlarged the horizon of ancient thought. The philosophers in the time of Cicero and Seneca had already risen from the national idea to that of the human race. It must not be supposed, however, that the universal religion sprang from the philosophic or religious syncretism of the later ages of Graeco-Roman civilisation. The dissolution of the national religions had preceded that of political nationalities, and, so far from creating anything universal, the morbid curiosity of minds denuded of all national tradition abandoned itself to individual superstitions the most exotic and monstrous. Christianity was born, not in Greece, in the schools, nor in Rome, at the foot of the throne of the Caesars, but in a race the narrowest, the most fanatical and intolerant that ever existed, and in the heart of a Son of Israel whom no extra-Palestinian influence seems ever to have reached.

Nowhere is a universal religion the fruit of an unconscious evolution, produced by the action of fatal and external laws. It presents itself everywhere as an individual creation, as the free and moral work of a few elect souls, in whom tradition by a profound crisis is purified and enlarged. This was the rôle of Confucius, of Buddha, of Socrates, of the prophets of Israel, of Mohammed in Arabia. All of them were reformers of the religion of their ancestors. . . . They did not discover the universal religion outside themselves, but in their consciousness and personal piety. Passing through their souls as through a filter, the traditional religion of their race was gradually clarified and freed from foreign or material elements, and it was found that, in the end, the new faith appeared the more human and universal as it had become more strictly religious, more inward, and more pure. . . . Not that all the ancient cults were capable of transformation or all the prophets equally inspired. Often the revelation would appear uncertain or incomplete. On only one point and in only one consciousness would it be seen to end in a clear and definitive conclusion. Progress implies selection. As we rise from one stage to another in the history of religious evolution we see the ranks enlightened and the number diminished of concurrent religions. At the lowest stage, the savage cults are almost innumerable. The great national or ethnic religions were much fewer. Only three are frankly universalist: Buddhism, Mohammedanism, and Christianity. And these three are universalist, if I may so say, in a very unequal degree.

Mohammedanism was far from being an original religion. The element which gives to it a higher moral and religious value came to it from Judaism and Christianity. Its monotheism, its horror of idolatry, the comparative purity of its ethics, have no other source, and, without paradox, it has been possible to represent it as an inferior form of Christianity accommodated to the needs and to the stature of semi-civilised Semitic peoples. But, alongside this Christian spiritualism it has conserved naturalistic elements, gross remnants of old Arab cults which, having made its fortune, perhaps, in its early days, now embarrass it and paralyse it. Moreover, in spite of its conquests, it has always remained an Oriental religion with Mecca as its centre and its head. If it would survive, it must reform itself; it must enter into the path of moral and intellectual progress, free itself from local superstitions, from its gross hopes, its hatred of the infidel, its doctrine of good works; in other words, it will have to cast off its old nature, and receive a new effusion of the Christian spirit. It can only become universal in so far as it approaches the moral principle of Christianity, in order, in the end, to become one with it.

Buddhism has a more profound originality, but it also is afflicted with an inward dualism which will ruin it. From the beginning there have been two Buddhisms: the one an esoteric philosophy for the use of sages convinced by experience of the vanity of all things, suffering from the essential evil of existence and aspiring to Nirvana. It is an unfruitful mysticism because it is Atheistic. The other is popular Buddhism, which sinks and dies into puerile superstitions and into the grossest polytheism. From which we may conclude that Buddhism only becomes universalist when it ceases to be a positive religion, and that where it still remains a religion it is anything but universalist.

With Christianity it is altogether different. The terms "universal religion" and "Christian religion" coincide so exactly that if a form of Christianity is not universalist on any side, on that particular side it ceases to be Christian. In fact there cannot here be either division or esoterism, nor consequently limitation or narrowness. We are here in the absolute freedom of spirit. Christ did not propound the theory of the unity of the human race; but He did something quite different and much better: He gave us the gospel. Between His gospel and the humanitarian philosophy there is all the difference that there is between abstraction and life, between idea and love. All men enter into the kingdom of God by the same door, and that door cannot be shut by any one; for it is the door of humility, of confidence, of self-renunciation, of the higher righteousness fulfilling itself by fraternal charity. Rank in that kingdom is determined by the measure of devotedness. The greatest is the one that humbles himself the most, and the only way of being master is to serve. In the religion of Jesus there is nothing religious but that which is authentically moral, and nothing moral in human life that is not truly religious. The perfect religion coincides with the absolute morality, and this naturally extends to and is obligatory on all mankind. Jesus not only proclaimed the only God, or even the God who is spirit, whose worship could not thenceforth be confined to anything material or particular in time and space: He showed us the Father who loves all His children with an equal affection, and desires to dwell in the humblest as well as in the highest consciousness. This divine

Fatherhood, in proportion as it is realised in our hearts, produces in them human brotherhood. The religious and the human ideals here join, no more to be separated. Having begun in the animal man, with the grossest form of religion, humanity finds itself completed in the perfect religion.

3. *Progress in Representations of the Divine*

To represent the divine, man has never had any but the resources which are in himself. These representations have varied therefore with the general progress of experience and of thought. . . . From beginning to end the evolution of religious images and notions is based on the idea of spirit. It is in this idea that the resemblance and the kinship of man to his God is based ; only by this can there be understanding, converse, harmony between them. Primitive religions, doubtless, are neither spiritualist nor materialist ; they are animistic. A simple animism gives to men their first conceptions. The child projects the life which animates him ; he endows the things around him with a personality similiar to his own. For him there is nothing dead or inert ; the world is peopled with living beings with which he contends, and talks, and is angry, to which he gives his love and his caresses. Do not let us smile too much at this simplicity. The latest steps of philosophy are rejoining our earliest thoughts. We are coming to see that in sum we know nothing but ourselves, that our science is but the projection of our consciousness without, and that it is solely on this condition that the world becomes intelligible to us. Man never worships anything purely material, anything that cannot hear and answer him. When he perceives that the object of his worship is inanimate, he thinks his god has deserted him, and he sets himself to pursue him. He usually finds him and retains him under other names and forms. By faith in ghosts, and by the memory of his dreams, he has learnt to double himself, and to oppose his will to his thought, his interior ego to his body, which he calls his house. He may easily quit this for another. Nothing is more ancient than the idea of the transmigration of souls. But at the same time he doubles the being of his gods; he distinguishes between the god and the object in which he habitually resides. This is the period at which *idolatry* begins. It will only be completed when the spirit-god has broken the bonds which bind him to its visible prison and its material image; when He shall speak who says that "God is a Spirit, and they that worship Him must worship Him in spirit and in truth." From that moment, mythology transforms itself into theology, and external rites into inward piety.

Necessarily polytheistic in its origins, religion tended nevertheless towards monotheism. The subordination which disciplined the heads of the tribes on earth also ranged the divinities under the authority of a supreme head. Force at first gave this supremacy. Zeus was the king of gods and men because he was stronger than all of them put together. This is the natural order of ideas. Force first imposed itself on weakness; then intelligence conquered force; lastly, justice and love, which is the supreme form and flower of righteousness, obtain supremacy over intelligence itself. The highest and the chiefest is no longer the strongest, or the wisest, but the best. In becoming moral, man has moralised his gods, who, in their turn, becoming models and authorities, have greatly helped to moralise the race.

It is very surprising that this evolution in the direction of moral monotheism did not complete itself in the Indo-European family. But the fact is that that family encountered an invincible barrier in the very nature of its primitive mythology. The

Greek and Hindu philosophers, no doubt, pushed the notion of God to that of His spirituality and unity, but they did not succeed in transforming the religion of their race. Their rational criticism had power to dissolve, but not to change. Their monotheism remained always an object of speculation more or less esoteric. When, in the second and third centuries of our era, in competition with Christianity, Graeco-Roman polytheism endeavoured to reach a sort of monotheism, it could only return to the most glorious mythus of its infancy, to the worship of the Sun, and raise it to supremacy among the symbols of their faith.

The transition from polytheism to monotheism was only made in Palestine and in the tradition of the Hebrews. There were two reasons for this, both of which bear witness to the divine vocation of that people: its religious predispositions and the powerful action of its prophets, of those men of God raised up in it from Moses to Christ. The desert is not monotheistic, as M. Renan was pleased at first to say, nor are nomads, shepherds, or freebooters nearer to the only God than sedentary and agricultural peoples. But, owing to the special turn of mind of the Hebrew family, its primitive polytheism, of which the plural, *elohim*, still reminds us, had an abstract character, and was reduced to a sort of anonymous plurality from which no divine genealogy could spring. All these elementary spirits, these *elohim* of the air, the earth, the waters, were so similar to each other that the thought of the Semite never succeeded in discerning and discriminating them. They entered into one another, and ended by forming a sort of collective and abstract power, analagous to that which is represented in our language by the word "divinity." Add to this that, by the idea of holiness, Jehovah, the national *elohim*, was equally separated from Nature, and that, gradually divested of all corporeal form, He was predestined to become the God of conscience, the invisible Creator of all things, the Judge and the rewarder of all human actions.

Neither these original predispositions, however, nor these general causes, account for the marvellous progress of the religion of Israel. The faith of the prophets is a creation of the moral order ; it is the work of individual consciousnesses, of the religious heroes whom the divine Spirit raised up in succession for more than a thousand years. We shall explain elsewhere this heroic and age-long struggle of the prophets of Jehovah against the customs, the tendencies, and even the temperament of their people. Suffice it here to indicate the constant direction of their efforts, the precision and the fixedness of their ideal, the power of the common inspiration that animated them, the vigorous and vivacious feeling in each one of them that makes their work divine and carries them beyond their individual thoughts and hopes. Like us they laboured on an infinitely vaster plane than they conceived.

But their conception of a divine ideal of righteousness still left God outside the consciousness. The image of His sanctity awakened in their souls the sense of sin and raised a tragic conflict between the human will enslaved by evil and the essentially inflexible law of God. God and man were found to be more profoundly separated by this moral antithesis of righteousness and sin than they had before been by the antithesis of strength and feebleness. How was this hostility to cease? A supreme revelation is about to respond to this cry of distress. God will become internal to the consciousness; He will manifest Himself, in man himself, as the principle of justification and salvation. He who was called *El, Allah*, the Mighty God, in patriarchal days,—He who from the times of Moses had been named *Jehovah*, the living God, the vigilant guardian of the Covenant,—will reveal

Himself as the Father in the filial consciousness of Jesus Christ. The revelation of love comes to crown the revelation of force and righteousness. God desires to dwell in human souls. The Heavenly Father lives within the Son of Man, and the dogma of the God-Man, interpreted by the piety of each Christian, not by the subtle metaphysics of the doctors and the schools, becomes the central and distinguishing dogma of Christianity. Do not spoil its religious meaning, leave the mystery intact, see what is wrapped up in it: the sin of man effaced, the ancient conflicts ended, harmony restored, the whole moral and spiritual life enrooted in the eternal life of God, the Divine Life shed abroad in the heart of man. Try to comprehend this consummation of the religious unity of the Divine and the human sought for, cried for, in the dim desire of consciousness, and you will also comprehend that, at this point of view, as at all the others, the precedent religious evolution found its *raison d'être* and its final aim in the soul and in the work of Christ. The orphaned human soul and the distant unknown God are re-united and embraced in filial love, to be no more divided or estranged.

4. *The History of Prayer*

The living expression of the relations of man to his God, prayer is the very soul of religion. It brings to God the miseries of man, and brings back to man the communion and the help of God. Nothing better reveals the worth and moral dignity of a religion than the kind of prayer it puts into the lips of its adherents. Now, progress is more apparent here than anywhere else. The savage beats his fetish when it is not complacent enough. The Christian in his greatest distresses repeats the prayer of Jesus in the Garden: "Father, not my will, but Thine be done!" What a long road man has travelled between these two extreme points of religion!

At the outset, prayer would seem to have had nothing religious in it except the vague trust which men placed in its efficiency. It was almost everywhere conceived and practised as a sort of constraint put by the worshipper on the will that he wished to master. There were mysterious syllables, which, pronounced correctly, would produce an irresistible effect. To the voice were added rites and ceremonies, *i.e.* gestures menacing or wheedling, whose object was to move the god and bind his will to that of man. Primitive stories and legends are full of this idea. Out of it sprang magic, sorcery, necromancy.

With the supernatural beings around him man does as with other neighbours. He seeks to induce them to help him, and that by the self-same means. There is very little respect in these primary relations. Ruse, violence, seduction by bribes or threats,—these are the forms of that strange supplication. It is human selfishness addressing itself naïvely to the selfishness of the gods. Regular contracts are made between these two egoisms, each of which arms itself against the other with the *Do ut des*. The god who fails in his promise deserves to be chastised, and privations, and even blows, do not fail to follow and punish his felony.

Sacrifice at first was merely a form of prayer. Man never approaches his superior or his master with empty hands. To secure his favour or appease his wrath he brings the offerings he believes to be the most agreeable. The gods, like mortals, *e.g.*, have need of nourishment. For them, therefore, are reserved the first-fruits of the human repast; libations, presents of honey and fine flour, the most luscious fruits, the most delicious viands. What difficulty man has had in believing in the goodness of his gods! He saw the effects of their anger in the evils which befell him, and if good fortune came to him he felt obliged to offer a sacrifice to turn aside the jealousy of higher powers. Was a god supposed to have been offended? They trembled for years beneath the strokes of his wrath; they offered in expiatory sacrifices all possible equivalents; they invented penances, humiliations, tortures, without being sure that the divine vengeance ever was appeased. These are universal religious phenomena.

The religious is so different from the moral sense that, at the outset, it exists by itself, and expresses itself in the most selfish and ferocious manner. How many crimes have been committed in the name of religion! with what baseness and sordidness has it not been sincerely connected! But here also we must note the new revelation made in the souls of prophets and of sages in order to raise the religion of naturalism to morality. Confucius, Buddha, the prophets of Israel, the philosophers of Greece, came simultaneously to feel that the true relation of man to God must be a moral relation, that righteousness is the only link which binds earth to heaven, that sacred words, rites, interested offerings, outward compensations, can do nothing, and mean nothing, the moment the religious man rises above the law of Nature and enters upon the higher life of the spirit. If God be righteous, there is only one means henceforth of putting one's self into harmony and peace with Him—to become like Him. Thus religion and morality were destined to approach each other and to penetrate each other more and more, until the perfect religion should be recognised by this sign: the highest piety under the form of the ideal morality. At bottom, Christianity has no other principle, and it is for this reason more than for any other that it is not only the highest form of religion, but the universal and final religion. "The absolute religion" and "the absolute moral life" are identical terms. The ancient dualism is surmounted in the unity of Christian consciousness.

It is not surprising, therefore, that prayer should, in its turn, be transformed, and that, having at first been the most violently interested act of life, it should come in the end to be a pure act of trust and self-abandonment, of disinterestedness the most religious and complete. Is there need of many words for a child to make its father understand? It is the heathen, says Jesus, who make many prayers. The Father knows your needs before you ask Him. It is a mark of unbelief to be anxious about food and raiment and the future. The essential thing is not to multiply petitions, but to live near Him and feel Him ever near. Is He not Almighty and all-good? Does He not love you better than you love yourselves? Does He not make all things work together for the good of His children? If trials come, or dangers threaten, what ought we to do? Submit to God, as Jesus did. What is such prayer as His but the defeat of egoism and the perfect liberation of the individual spirit in the feeling of its plenary union with God?

Such was the prayer of Jesus. It did not consist in an outward flow of words, but in a constant, silent state of soul which made Him say in turning towards His Father: "I know that Thou hearest me always." Confidence increases with renunciation. Admirable progress of religion! Sublime reversal of rôles! At the beginning the ambition of the pious man was to bend the Divine will to his own; at the end his peace, his happiness, is to subordinate his wishes and desires to the will of a Father who knows how to be gracious, righteous, perfect!

There is another aspect of this progress. In all religions there is a double gamut of feeling: the one, which rules in primitive religions, and whose dominant note is fear and sadness; the other, which prevails in the end, in which the dominant note is confidence and joy. It is a natural effect of the progressive victory of the religious consciousness gradually surmounting the contradictions in the midst of which it is born and developed. At the outset, man, alone and defenceless, finds no fewer enemies in heaven than on earth. He feels as if surrounded by hostile and mysterious powers before which he cringes in fear, awaiting their decisions with respect to him. But everything changes when there rises within his soul the luminous dawn of the moral revelation of God. With the darkness, vanish all the frightful phantoms of the night. In the God whom he adores he sees his own interior law glorified and become henceforth the supreme law of things. That law of righteousness is, at bottom, a law of love. Nothing can trouble me any more except the sense of my own failure—that is, of my own sin, which alone can separate me from the very principle of righteousness and life. But, see, justice manifests itself as justifying grace! God gives it as He gives life to those who thirst for it. Reconciliation is complete. The orphan has found his Father; the Father, His child. The sinner, trembling, begins his prayer, prostrated; he ends it upright, with the confidence and freedom of a child that feels itself at home within the Father's house. The Gospel bids us to rejoice; it makes of joy an obligation, while distrust and sadness are the marks of selfishness and unbelief.

5. Conclusion

Such has been the course of religion through the centuries of human history, and amid the complex and confused development of particular faiths. The progress has not been on a straight line and by successive additions, as in the scientific sphere. Religious evolution is more like the evolution of art, in which the experience of the past is only fruitful when translated by a higher inspiration and a mightier creative force. There are periods of recrudescence of the religious sentiment in which the passions of a past that seemed to have been abolished are revived. These are the times of superstition. There are also periods of religious inertia, when the soul seems to empty itself of its eternal content, and divert itself into a frivolous activity and a superficial wisdom. These are the ages of incredulity. Lastly, there are epochs of crisis and confusion, in which mingle religious traditions the most diverse, and currents of thought the most contrary. We must pass over all these accidents and vicissitudes. In the religious evolution of humanity there is a sequence, an order, a progress which, in spite of all interruptions and reactions, manifest themselves as soon as we rise high enough to embrace it in its vast entirety.

· · · · · ·

A few years ago there assembled in Chicago what the Americans called the Parliament of Religions. The official representatives of all the principal religions of the new world and the old met together under a common feeling of religious brotherhood. They did not discuss the value of their rites or dogmas; their object was to approach each other, to edify each other, and, for the first time in the world's history, to present the spectacle of a universal religious communion. When it came to the point, three things became clear: first, the common name under which they were able to call upon God—the Father; secondly, the Lord's Prayer was adopted and recited by all; thirdly, Christ Himself, apart from all theological definition, was unanimously recognised and venerated as the Master and Initiator of the higher religious life.

In my own consciousness, this practical demonstration is completed. I can hardly help being religious; but if I am seriously to be religious I can only be so under the Christian form. I can hardly help praying; but if I desire to pray, if moral anguish or intellectual doubt constrain me to seek some form of prayer that I can use in all sincerity, I never find but these words: "Our Father which art in heaven." Lastly, I may disdain the inner life of the soul, and divert myself from it by the distractions of science, art, and social life; but if, wearied by the world of pleasure or of toil, I wish to find my soul again and live a deeper life, I can accept no other guide and master than Jesus Christ, because, in Him alone, optimism is without frivolity, and seriousness without despair.

BOOK SECOND

CHRISTIANITY

CHAPTER I

HEBRAISM, OR THE ORIGINS OF THE GOSPEL

To understand Christianity we should need to see clearly and in one view the link which connects it with the religious evolution of mankind, the living originality by which it is distinguished, the succession and the character of the forms it has assumed. Such are the three points which we shall take up in turn. We must begin with its origins.

There is never a complete break in the chain of history. Every phenomenon arises in its place and at its time. It has its antecedents, which prepare it and *condition* it. However new Christianity may have been, it is no exception to the rule. It springs from the tradition of Israel by an evident affiliation. The old theology did not dissimulate this kinship of origin; it rather exaggerated it. The Christian Church made the Bible of the Jews the first part of its own. The writings of the prophets were placed in the sacred volume before those of the apostles, as if to intimate that the one could not be understood without the other. *Novum Testamentum in Vetere latet; Vetus in Novo patet.* At bottom, this old adage of the schoolmen is true. It is an excellent rule of biblical exegesis to trace the primary Christian ideas to their Hebraic root, and to regard as foreign and adventitious those which are not attached to it. If there is nothing essential in the New Testament the germ of which is not to be found in the Old, there is nothing truly fruitful in the Old which has not passed into the New. Such is the historical sequence and connection that we must respect and follow. The study of the religion of Israel is the natural introduction to the study of Christianity. The only point to be considered here is how the one was preparatory to the other.[1]

1. *Prophetism*

The miracle of the history of Israel is Prophetism. In this is to be found the incomparable force by which the religious evolution we may trace in its annals was effected.

---

[1] Two non-essential sections have here been omitted, one on *The Sacred History*, the other on *The Nation.*—Trans.

But first let me explain what I understand by this word evolution, and let me eliminate from it the fatalistic sense too often given to it. If by evolution you mean a necessary and unconscious process, a mechanical and continuous movement, which, without either effort or danger, causes light to spring out of darkness, good from evil, and raises a people or a race from a lower to a higher form of life, you incur the reproach of confounding the laws of the moral world with those of the physical order; you will be condemned to falsify history in general and to understand nothing of the history of Israel in particular. In the moral and religious progress which constitutes the singular originality of that history, there is nothing facile, nothing that can be logically deduced from the natural predispositions of the nation. No doubt the prophets were the children of the nation and intimately connected with it; but the inspiration which breathes in them, raises them and animates them, is something entirely different from the ethnic genius of their race. The contrast is so great that it amounts to contradiction. The race, in Israel, as in Moab, or among the Edomites or Philistines, had its interpreters and prophets. But these were not the prophets of conscience. They flatter the people; they do not elevate them. They are found to be false prophets. The others, the witnesses for the righteous, holy God, only brought Hebraism to the consciousness of its religious vocation by a sæcular and painful struggle against hereditary idolatry and immorality. This was not a collective evolution, but an essentially individualist reform; it was a moral creation continually interrupted and compromised; it was a work of faith and will. Each prophet enters into the conflict and utters his cry of battle and reform as if he were alone, responsible only to the God who has sent him, and yet all of them succeed each other and pursue the same design, because they are all obedient to the same identic inspiration. They fight against all; against the multitude that cannot break away from custom and from prejudice; against the priests who have always from the beginning made of the priesthood a *métier* and of oracles a merchandise; against kings whose vanity, whose crimes, and whose exactions they denounce; against the great and rich oppressors of the weak and poor. They speak in the name of Jehovah, because Jehovah speaks in their consciousness. That is the origin of the prophetic spirit. It is a divine ferment which, perpetuating itself, becoming clearer, stronger, from generation to generation, gradually raises and transmutes the heavy mass of primitive Semitism. No, this is not the work of time and Nature, unless you see God at work in time, and, beneath this word Nature, by the side of realised and manifested forces you perceive the hidden and immeasurable virtualities which ferment in it and carry it beyond itself into the higher life of liberty and love. In the apparition of these prophets, in the energy of their faith, in the boldness of their words, there is a positive revelation of a new world, the revelation of a religious ideal which, after divesting itself, in the gospel of Christ, of every national element, will naturally become the faith and consolation of humanity.

. . . . .

The education of the people of God had been a long and laborious work; besides the preaching of the prophets, it had needed repeated catastrophes in which the nationality of Israel had perished, as if the spirit could not free itself save by the annihilation of the matter that had from the outset grossly closed it in. When in the age of Cyrus we see the poor remnants of Benjamin and Judah return from Babylon, they are no longer a people; they are already almost a

Church. The religious Law is now fixed. It enshrines the life, the ideas, the ethics and the ritual, the minute practices and precautions, which will for ever separate the Jew from all the other nations, and maintain him in a state of legal purity and high morality in the midst of universal corruption. It is the beginning of Pharisaism. In it the spirit of prophetic piety deteriorates, hardens, freezes. Nevertheless, when we think of the progress that had been accomplished, when we think of the distance that separates this rigid monotheism and this rigorous law from the old hard, cruel, sometimes impure Semitic cults, the prophets' work in Israel will appear to us in its immense proportions and immortal worth.

2. *The Dawn of the Gospel*

But Prophetism was not to end in the Talmud. The Isaiahs and Jeremiahs were to have other heirs and successors than the Pharisees and the sons of the Synagogue. Prophetism had in it the promise and the germ of a higher and more human religion. The prophets had accents which their immediate successors in history seem never to have heard. They attacked nothing with more vehemence than formalistic piety or practical religion divorced from righteousness. Listen to

Amos, as he makes Jehovah utter words like these: "I hate, I despise your feast days," etc. (Amos v. 21 *et seq.*); or to Isaiah on the same theme in his first chapter. Hosea declares that heart-piety and mercy are better than sacrifices. Jeremiah predicts the time when God will make a new Covenant with His people, and write His laws in their hearts, instead of on tables of stone. Or think of Elijah in the cave of Horeb. Fatigued with fighting, almost in despair, the terrible adversary of Baal, who had just had 450 of the priests of Baal put to death, has retired to the mountains and is asleep in a cave. You know the narrative (1 Kings xix. 9-13). The still small voice! Is there in all the Bible a finer image containing a profounder thought? What is this supreme revelation of the God of Israel but an apparition by anticipation of the God of the Gospel? And the still, small voice, "the sound of gentle stillness," what is it but the first faint accents of the gracious, tender words: "Come unto Me, all ye that labour and are heavy laden, and I will give you rest. Take My yoke upon you, and learn of Me; for I am meek and lowly in heart: and ye shall find rest unto your souls. For My yoke is easy, and My burden is light" (Matt. xi. 28-30).

Beneath the breathings of this creative inspiration the religion of legal righteousness and rigorous retributions is softened into the religion of love. The God who punishes becomes the God who pardons and restores. Beneath the tears of the poor, the vanquished, the afflicted in Israel the gospel of divine compassion germinated and sprang up. What tones of tenderness are heard in the later prophets, the prophets of consolation, properly so called. "Comfort ye, comfort ye My people. Speak ye comfortably to Jerusalem. Say unto her that her warfare is accomplished, that her iniquity is pardoned." Read the chapter through (Is. xl.), and the forty-second and the sixty-sixth, and Psalms xxiii. and ciii. Such words as these announce and prepare the way for the great religious revolution called by Jesus the New Covenant. The relations between God and the human soul are in course of being changed. From the beginning, a pact existed between Jehovah and His people; a compact expressed and guaranteed in a Law on which depended the destiny of the nation and of the individual. The Covenant has become more inward and profound. To the law of strict remunerations is now joined a bond of love. Between God and His people the relations are those of Husband and wife. The wife has proved unfaithful to Him who had loved her, who had found her poor and naked in the desert, and had been desirous to enrich her. She has followed other gods. Jehovah, by the mouth of His messengers, covers her with reproaches, in order to excite her to repentance; but He has learnt to pity, and, in the end, He pardons. The more the nation's miseries are multiplied, the more its tears flow on the soil of alien lands, the more His heart is melted in Him and the tenderer become His words. "Can a woman forget her sucking child, that she should not have compassion on the son of her womb? yea, she may forget, yet will not I forget thee" (Is. xlix. 15).

The idea beneath these words is the Christian idea. God loves His people with a boundless love. His mercy extends infinitely beyond the sins of the children of men. In the consciousness of the great unknown prophet whom we call the second Isaiah, we see sketched, five centuries beforehand, the drama of repentance and forgiveness, which Jesus, in profounder and yet simpler words, sums up for all mankind in the Parable of the Prodigal Son.

The long period of affliction and of misery between the Captivity and the Advent of the Christ is like a time of painful gestation, during which, in the bosom of the Hebraic tradition, fecundated by the spirit of the prophets, was prepared in obscurity the gospel of the Beatitudes and of the Parables. What a revolution! The ancient theocratic law promised to the righteous length of days and great abundance of material goods. The friends of Job regarded him as criminal because they saw him in adversity. The problem of human destiny appeared to the later prophets as less simple and more tragic. "Why do the wicked prosper?" is the question ever on their lips. "Why do the righteous suffer?" This spectacle has become so constant that the correlation of the words has been reversed. "Rich and wicked" in the Psalmists, and in the second Isaiah, are equivalent terms. "Poor and afflicted" are synonymous with "the righteous" and "the friends of God." Riches and high looks are the signs of malediction; humility, poverty, persecution, tears, are the marks of piety and the pledges of divine affection. It was at this time that the words were born that edified the early Christians: "God resisteth the proud, but giveth grace to the humble." Gather together in a common hope this family of little ones, of the defeated and unhappy ones whose hearts were crushed and whose eyes were filled with tears, and you have the true people of God, the heirs of all the promises, the "little flock" to whom it is the Father's pleasure to give the kingdom. It was from their ranks that was to come the "Man of Sorrows," who should be scourged and put to death for the sins of His people. The religion of suffering is born. For the suffering of "the Servant of Jehovah," in whom is no iniquity, cannot be the chastisement of His own crimes; it will henceforth be accepted as the necessary part that fraternal solidarity imposes on the best for the redemption of the rest. A tender, fragile flower, a bud as yet scarce opened in the writings of the prophets, this thought will expand into the Gospel and become the religion of mankind.

Pity joined to a severe ideal of righteousness in the notion of God; morality introduced into religion by the subordination of rites to rectitude of heart and will; hope of a future of peace and happiness by the realisation of righteousness: these are the three great ideas bequeathed by Prophetism to the Gospel. This heritage is a rich and lovely one, but it must not be over-estimated or misunderstood. We are still a long way off the Gospel. The thought of the prophets did not go beyond the narrow limits of a national Messianism; it remained Jewish, not only by its forms and symbols, but also by the religious privilege which is to guard the people of Israel in the future as in the past. The destiny of humanity is still bound up with the destiny of Jerusalem, and the triumph of the Jews implies the partial or total defeat and subjection of the Gentiles in the days of the Messiah and after they are admitted into the kingdom of God. The saints of Israel are the children of the household; the heathen may enter, and even share in the felicity which fills them, but only as servants and tributaries.

It should also be noted that, in the theology of the prophets, the object of Jehovah's love is not the individual as a moral being, but the chosen people. Only the nation counts in the eyes of the Eternal. In its deliverance and triumph the citizens find salvation. . . . There is something great and thrilling in this Messianic doctrine. It elevated the soul of a people and of a religion to the point of the sublime. It is something to have given hope to a defeated people and a dying world. In this doctrine also we may note this admirable trait: this national triumph is identified with the advent of righteousness to all the earth. Nor have the hopes of Israel been belied. The dream of the prophets was realised in ways of which they did not think, but in a manner not less marvellous. The descendants of Japhet lodge to-day beneath the tents of the children of Shem, and our eyes may see the day approaching when the ancient promise made to Abraham and his seed shall be fulfilled, and all the families of the earth be blessed in Him.

Between the religion of the prophets and the religion of Jesus, however, there is one more barrier to be broken down. In the "Kingdom of God," the idea of the nation must give place to the idea of humanity. The universal God must be represented as the immanent God, as present in every human soul. His seat and temple could not be in Jerusalem or in Palestine; it could only be in pure and humble hearts. A supreme crisis was necessary. The Hebrew nation must perish in order to free the human conscience from its Jewish yoke. A divine flower had been formed in the heart of Prophetism; but it would have been a barren ornament, had there not been deposited in its calix a living and a fruitful germ. The transformation of the piety of the prophets into a purely moral creation and a Covenant really new with God, this was the work of Jesus Christ. That is why Jesus is " He that should come," He whom the prophets half unconsciously desired, He in whom, to the profit of all mankind, was completed the religious development of Israel. Its whole history ends in Jesus. Apart from Him the inspiration of the prophets dies into rabbinical Talmudism or wanders into the vagaries and delirium of the apocalypses. After giving birth to the Gospel, Judaism dries up and withers like a tree that has borne its fruit, and whose season is past.

CHAPTER II

THE ESSENCE OF CHRISTIANITY

1. *The Problem*

WE come at last to Christianity. What is its principle or essence? This question must be answered or we cannot judge of it aright.

Now, during the eighteen centuries of its history, Christianity has taken so many and such various forms, it has received so many developments in every sense, it has become a thing so rich and luxuriant, that it is far from easy to discover beneath this thick growth of institutions, dogmas, ceremonies, and devotions the tap-root of the tree from which it all has sprung, and from which it still derives its nutriment. It would be next to useless to interrogate the Churches. They would each answer according to their official theologies and Confessions of Faith. This, they would say, is the essence of Christianity. The Catholics would say it is the institution and infallible authority of the Church, because everything rests on this first foundation, and because no one can be in Christian truth who is outside the Church. The Protestants would not be agreed: one would propose the dogma of Justification by Faith; another the authority of Scripture; a third the metaphysical divinity and the eternal pre-existence of Jesus Christ, under the pretext that they could not conceive the possibility of the subsistence of Christianity without these dogmas. In entering on this examination we enter on an interminable dispute.

The problem, happily, is simplified for the historian and the psychologist. In asking what is the principle of Christianity, what do we wish to know? Simply what it is that makes a Christian a Christian. We desire to ascertain what is the inward element, present in the soul, which compensates, at need, for the absence or defect of all the rest, and which, being wanting, cannot be supplied or compensated for by anything else. In short, we want to get at the religious experience which determines and marks out the consciousness of all Christians, which makes them members of one moral family, and which makes them to be recognised as such in spite of differences of times and place, of language and of culture, of rites and even of beliefs. To seize this common feature there is no need of polemics; all we need is a little history and psychology.

In history, Christianity offers itself to us as the term and crown of the religious evolution of humanity. In the consciousness of the Christian it is something more; it there reveals itself as the perfect religion. How must we understand this perfection? Is it the perfection of a complete system of supernatural knowledge, of a religious science which would have been strange to former generations, and which was shared by Christians alone? In no wise. If there are enlightened Christians, there are many who are very ignorant. And yet they are all Christians by one and the same principle, which is entirely independent of degrees of culture. No Christian will maintain that his knowledge is perfect. They all agree with St. Paul that at present it is very imperfect. We see divine things dimly. What, then, do they affirm who say with so much assurance that Christianity is the perfect religion? They affirm that, religion not being an idea but a relation to God, the perfect religion is the perfect realisation of their relation to God and of God's relation to them. And this is not, on their part, a theoretical speculation; it is the immediate and practical result of their inward experience. They feel that their religious need is entirely satisfied, that God has entered with them, and they with Him, into a relation so intimate and so happy that, in the matter of practical religion, not only can they imagine nothing, but that they can desire nothing above it or beyond. They simply set themselves to realise more fully and more effectually in themselves this supreme relation, this piety whose principle is immanent to themselves; they know that in it they have the germ of perfect spiritual development and eternal life. This is why they affirm without the slightest doubt that Christianity is the ideal and perfect religion, the definitive religion of humanity.

Such is the first affirmation of the Christian consciousness. Here is the second.

This perfect relation between God and my soul, this supreme religious good, this kind of piety which constitutes my joy and strength, which enlightens, renovates, sustains my whole inner life, does not date from myself, and I well know that it is not my own virtue that has created it. Nor can I refer the origin of it to my parents, although I may perhaps have received it through them or through my teachers; nor to my Church, although I still remain its catechumen; for parents, teachers, churches, will acknowledge, with myself, that they have only transmitted that which they themselves received. Remounting thus the living chain of Christian experiences, I reach a first experience, a creative and inaugural experience, which has made possible and engendered all the rest. That experience was realised in the consciousness of Jesus Christ. I affirm, then, not only that Christ was the author of Christianity, but that the first germ of it was formed in His inner life, and that in that life, first of all, that divine revelation was made which, repeating and multiplying itself, has enlightened and quickened all mankind. Christianity is therefore not only the ideal, but an historical religion, inseparably connected not only with the maxims of morality and with the doctrines of Jesus, but with His person itself, and with the permanent action of the new spirit which animated Him, and which lives from generation to generation in His disciples.

These are the two affirmations, equally immediate and equally essential, of every Christian consciousness. Now, the whole theological problem is how to reconcile the two. How can that which is ideal and perfect be realised in history?

How can that which is historical be held to be ideal and eternal? Does it not seem as if these attributes were contradictory and exclusive of each other, and that Christianity could not become an ideal religion without severing all its links with a particular history, or that if it would remain an historical religion it must renounce all pretensions to absolute perfection? On the other hand, these two attributes, are they not equally necessary to it? How can it subsist if it obeys the formal and summary logic which summons us to choose between them? Will it be anything more than a speculative philosophy if cut off from its historic tradition? Will it continue to inspire me with confidence, will it place me in security, if it ceases to appear to me to be the perfect and definitive religion?

Theology, from the beginning, has had no other task; at all events, it has had no task more arduous or pressing than that of reconciling these two data. There have always been two tendencies amongst theologians corresponding to two families of minds: the *Idealist* tendency—that of Origen and his emulators, which puts the emphasis on ideas and constructs a religious metaphysic or gnosis, which of necessity rationalises dogma, and for which history is but a temporary envelope, a sort of external and sensible illustration ; and the *Realist* tendency, represented by the genius of Tertullian, which, obeying an opposite instinct, materialises ideas, gives an anthropomorphic body to everything, even to God, deifies phenomena, and changes contingent history into an eternal metaphysic. From these two tendencies, perpetual and parallel, have issued the two solutions given by Rationalism and by Orthodoxy to the problem as to the essence of Christianity.

The first finds that essence in a few simple truths of reason or of consciousness, which are of all time and all lands, and which impose themselves on every man by their own natural evidence. Jesus of Nazareth was the preacher and the martyr of these truths ; but it is clear that His personality is no more essential to Christianity than that of Plato is to his philosophy. Only, mind, in thus severing itself from Christ the Christian Religion ceases to be positive and becomes an abstract and dead doctrine ; it loses its religious pith and power.

Orthodoxy, whether Catholic or Protestant, avoids this reef but strikes upon another. In making of Christ the Second Person of the Eternal Trinity, the Son of the Father, consubstantial and equal, it removes Him from history and transports Him into metaphysics. But thus to deify history is also in a fashion to destroy it. The dogma annuls the limited, contingent, and human character of the appearance of Jesus of Nazareth. His life loses all reality. We have no longer a man before our eyes, although the Church, theoretically, maintains the humanity of Christ alongside His divinity. This fatally absorbs everything. We have only a deity walking in the midst of His contemporaries, hidden beneath a human figure. The traditional Christology has been so incurably Docetic that it has been practically impossible, from this point of view, to write a serious Life of Jesus without falling into the heresy at once modern and semi-pagan of *Kenosis*, the theory according to which the pre-existent and eternal deity commits suicide by incarnating Himself in order gradually to be re-born and find Himself God again at the end of His human life.

Can this strait be crossed? Is there a passage between Scylla and Charybdis? Not so long as you cling to the intellectualist conception which forms the error common to both Rationalism and Orthodoxy, and ensures their final failure. If the essence of Christianity lies in the revelation of natural truths or supernatural dogmas, the problem is insoluble. All Apologetics will inevitably dash themselves to pieces against the insurmountable contradiction that they will soon encounter. Strauss's argumentation, which the philosophers do not cease to repeat, and which the theologians pretend not to hear, springs into one's mind. So far from weakening it, the historical studies of the past half century have only added sharpness to its edge. "The idea does not pour all its riches into a single individual. The Absolute does not descend into history. It is against all analogy that the fulness of perfection should be met with at the outset of any evolution whatsoever; those who place it at the origin of Christianity are victims of the same illusion as the ancients, who placed the Golden Age at the beginning of human history."

Before going further it may be convenient to estimate the strength and weakness of this famous dilemma, and to inquire how we may escape from it. The traditional theology succumbs to it. But this only proves that that theology needs reforming. Let us place ourselves at a different point of view, and examine for a moment the idea of perfection which serves as the premise to Strauss's reasoning. When he speaks of the total or plenary perfection which cannot be found in the first link of an historical chain, he doubtless means a quantitative perfection—that is to say, a complete collection of virtues, merits, and faculties the numerical addition of which makes the notion entire. Now, from this point of view, Strauss's observation is incontestable. Neither the perfection of science comprising all scientific discoveries, nor the perfection of civilisation embracing all the progress and all the forms of human life, are ever found or could be found at the beginning or at any given moment in the course of history. One individual, however great, could not exhaust the life or labour of the species so as to render evolution useless. But have you noticed that this idea of perfection is contradictory, and therefore chimerical? Under the category of quantity or of extension there could be no real perfection either for the individual or for the species. No sooner is anything that can be counted or measured conceived than the mind instantly conceives something greater. There is no such thing as perfect number. Here therefore it is needful to make an essential distinction. We must distinguish between the quantity and the quality, or rather, the intensity, of being. Now, between the degrees of both these things there is not the slightest relation, nor consequently any common measure. And that which is true in the one becomes false in the other. Take a cubic metre of stone, multiply it by a thousand or a million, you will still have the same stone—that is to say, there is not more true reality in a million cubic metres of stone than there is in one. But let a bit of moss spring up in a fissure in that stone; in that bit of living moss there is more being, or, if you will, being of a higher quality than that of a whole mass of rocks. Still, do not forget that it needed a germ to produce it, and that this germ was a sort of positive perfection in relation to all inorganic matter, whose last end is life. This is why we may boldly say that evolution is not the cause of anything; that no development ever gives more than what is hidden in the new germ which engenders it; that a hundred thousand imbeciles do not make a man of genius, and that if man descended from a monkey all the monkeys in creation put together do not make up one human consciousness. From this synthetic point of view, it will no longer seem contradictory, but natural, and in full accordance with the analogies of history, that we should meet in the person of the Founder of Christianity that perfect relation to God, that perfection of piety which every Christian still experiences within himself, and which he declares he has drawn from communion with Him.

Lastly, let us fortify ourselves, and finish this brief statement of this somewhat novel view with Pascal's pregnant words. There are, he says, three orders of greatness. From all bodies put together you could not extract one thought, if there were not first a mind to conceive it. From all thoughts you could not draw a single movement of charity, if there were not there a heart to produce and feel it. So far from needing to manifest themselves by the same attributes, these various kinds of greatness are absolutely independent of each other and even incommensurable. That which makes one shine forth would diminish or obscure the others. Alexander came with a pomp which dazzled the eyes and astonished the imaginations of mere carnal men. Archimedes had no need of the pomp of Alexander in order to impress the minds of men; his greatness, purely intellectual, was of an altogether different order. And, so, the Christ did not come with the *éclat* of Alexander or Archimedes. His greatness is of another order still. It is in fact so different that neither the glory of the conqueror nor the potency of genius would add anything to it, and that it had need, the better to shine forth to all, to appear in lowliness and humiliation. Therefore He was humble, patient, gentle, holy towards God, merciful towards man, terrible to all the hosts of darkness. Without sin, without external goods, without the productions of science, He was in His own order. Oh, with what pomp, with what transcendent magnificence, did He appear to the eyes of the heart that discerns true wisdom!

2. *The Christian Principle*

We must therefore come to the religious consciousness of Jesus Christ as to the fountain-head from which the Christian stream has flowed. It is certain that we shall find in it the principle and essence of Christianity itself, for it would be too paradoxical to maintain that the Master alone was excluded from the benefit of the religion that He has bequeathed to all His disciples. No; we may affirm in all security that the principle of Christianity was at first the very principle of the consciousness of Christ. To determine the one will be to define the other.

What we call the religious consciousness of a man is the feeling of the relation in which he stands, and wills to stand, to the universal principle on which he knows himself to depend, and with the universe in which he sees himself to be a part of one great whole. If then we would know exactly what was the essential element in the consciousness of Jesus, what was the distinctive characteristic of His piety, we must ask in what relation did He feel Himself to stand towards God and towards the universe.. The answer will be neither difficult nor uncertain. If there are matters on which the true thought of the Master remains obscure, nothing shines out with more evidence and continuity through all His teaching and His life than the religious attitude of His soul towards God and man.

He felt Himself to be in a filial relation towards God, and He felt that God was in a paternal relation towards Him. The name of Father that He gives to God continually, exclusively, uniquely; the name of Son that He takes to Himself; the nature of His adoration; the form of His prayer; the motive of His devoted obedience even unto death; the way in which He works His cures, hails His first successes, accepts the apparent failure of His work, and explains the incredulity of His people,—all announce, manifest, and confirm that intimate relation, that communion and union of spirit, by which a father prolongs his life in the life of his child, and the child feels himself to live by the life of his father. This was clearly the essential element in His consciousness, the distinctive and original feature of His piety; it is also the principle and essence of Christianity.

That which we observe in the consciousness of Jesus we find in the experience of all Christians. They are Christians exactly in proportion as the filial piety of Jesus is reproduced in them. They are recognised by this unique but sufficient sign, by the confidence with which they call God their Father, abandoning themselves to His love for all that regards their present or future destiny, and living a life of self-renunciation and of devotion to the good of others. All whose inner life has been raised from the region of selfishness and pride to the higher realm of love and life in God,—who have found in that profound conversion, together with the pardon and oblivion of their past, the germ of a higher life,—of the perfect, and, by consequence, eternal life, are the true religious posterity of Christ; they reproduce His spirit, continue His work, and are as dependent upon Him and as like Him religiously as are the descendants of an ancestor whose blood and whose life have not ceased for an instant to flow in their veins.

This feeling, filial in regard to God, fraternal in regard to man, is that which makes a Christian, and consequently it is the common trait of all

Christians. It should be added that this principle of Christianity admirably corresponds to the two fundamental affirmations of the Christian consciousness already established. The contradiction that appeared to us so menacing is thus resolved and reconciled. On the one hand, Christianity, by this filial union with God, is seen to be the ideal and perfect religion; on the other, it appears as a real fact in the consciousness of Jesus Christ, so that this religious reality comes to us with the imperative character of the ideal. Through prejudice men may neglect religion, but if they desire to have one they can neither desire nor imagine a relation at once closer and more moral, more sacred and more joyous, freer and more trustful, than that which was inaugurated in the filial consciousness of Jesus Christ. What can they have in the shape of life superior to the life of perfect and reciprocal affection,—God giving Himself to man and realising in him His paternity, man giving himself to God without fear, and realising in Him his humanity? Is not religious evolution accomplished when these two terms, God and man, opposed to each other at the origin of conscious life on earth, interpenetrate each other till they reach the moral unity of love, in which God becomes interior to man and lives in him, in which man becomes interior to God and finds in God the full expansion of his being? Christianity is therefore the absolute and final religion of mankind.

At the same time, this filial piety in the person of Jesus and His followers is an observable phenomenon; so that the ideally perfect religion has manifested itself from the beginning as an historical and positive religion. It is not an abstract ideal, a theoretical doctrine, floating above humanity, but a principle and a tradition of new life, an inexhaustibly fruitful germ inserted in human life to raise it, not in idea but in fact, to a higher form. That which the first human consciousness was on earth, separating itself from its maternal animality, and bringing with it the kingdom of man, the initiative consciousness of Christ, issuing from the bosom of antique humanity, has been, and it has founded on our humble planet the kingdom of God, the kingdom, *i.e.*, of free, pure spirit, of righteousness and love. We are no longer therefore in face of a rational doctrine or a speculative view, but of a positive force, of a power of life with which no one can break (I do not say in form and from without, but in fact and in the inner man) without at the same time breaking with the higher life of spirit as well as with all hope and joy, and health of soul.

. .

3. *The Gospel of Jesus*

The Christian principle appears in its simple and naked form, in the form of feeling and of inspiration, in the soul of Jesus. It is described, explained, expanded, in His Gospel. The Gospel in fact is merely the popular translation and the immediate application of the principle of the piety of Jesus in the social *milieu* in which He lived. Everything springs from His filial consciousness as a natural and wonderful efflorescence: His messianic vocation, His twofold ministry of preaching and healing, His deeds and His discourses, His ethics and His doctrine, the absolute gift of Himself in life and death. We must place ourselves at this luminous centre if we would see the rest dart forth like rays. In it is found the inner, living unity of His teaching and His destination. He promulgates no law or dogma; He founds no official institution. His intention is quite different: He wishes, before everything else, to awaken the moral life, to rouse the soul from its inertia, to break its chains, to lighten its burden, to make it active, free, and fruitful. He regards His work as finished when He has communicated His life, His piety, to a few poor consciousnesses that He found asleep and dead. Never man spake like this man, because never had man less concern about what we call "orthodoxy"—that is, about abstract and accurate formulas. He prefers the language of the people to the language of the schools ; He makes use of images, parables, paradoxes, of current and traditional ideas, of every form of expression which, taken literally, is the most inadequate in the world, but which, on the other hand, is the most living and stimulating. Each of His sentences or parables is enclosed in a hard shell that has to be broken before you can get at the kernel. Jesus wished to force His hearers to interpret His words, because He called them to an inward, personal, autonomous activity, because He wished to put an end to the religion of the letter and of rites, and to found the religion of the spirit. Even now, he that does not give himself to this labour of interpretation and assimilation in reading the Gospel,—he who does not penetrate through the letter and the form to the inspiration and the inmost consciousness of the Master,—cannot understand or profit by His teaching. He who does not collaborate with Him while listening to Him, who does not pierce through His words to His soul, will come away empty. He only gives to those who have, or at least desire to have. He only leads the seeker to the truth. He only pardons those who repent, or comforts those who mourn, or fills the hungerers and the thirsters after righteousness.

Such is the character of His Gospel. We cannot here set forth its contents; we can only note the religious attitude of Jesus with regard to things and men, to Nature and Society.

At peace with God, Jesus found Himself at peace with the universe. The idea of Nature, that formidable screen erected between ourselves and God, destroying hope and quenching prayer, did not exist for Him. Nature—that was the Will of His Father. He submitted to it with confidence and joy, whereas we submit to it with desperate resignation. He did not feel Himself to be an orphan or an exile in the world; He conducted Himself in it with ease and in security, not as a slave, but as a son in the house which the Father filled with His presence. It is the Father that directs all things; He makes His sun to shine upon the evil and the good; He watches over the sparrows; He clothes the lilies of the field; He gives life and food, the body and raiment; He notices the work we have to do, the trials we must bear. He never leaves us to ourselves. His spirit vivifies and fortifies our own. He is at the origin of our life and at the end. We are ever in the Father's hands.

The outlook of Jesus, it is true, is not our own. He shared the outlook of His race and time. . . . But His filial piety did not depend upon His knowledge of the universe. The amount of culture does not count in this order of feelings. Irreligion was not less easy or less frequent then than now, and if His outlook on the universe was narrower, it must not be imagined that it was less full of scandalous fatalities, of moral difficulties, of rude shocks to piety and faith. The world of the apocalypses, which was the world in which Jesus had to live and act, was not less full of mysteries and terrors than our own. His filial piety alone gave Him the means and strength by which to overcome them. The duty of man, He considered, was to change his heart rather than to change the order of things, *i.e.* the will of God. There is no trace of sorcery or magic or the appetite for miracles in the prayer He taught to His disciples. At bottom it amounts to this: "Our Father, let Thy will be done!" His heart-obedience was composed half of childlike confidence, half of heroic renunciation. In face of His trials He submitted without weakness and without complaint, and in face of death He breathed the prayer of faith, the only one that still remains to us: "Father, into Thy hands I commend my spirit."

In face of the universe and its laws the individual ego is necessarily called on to submit and to renounce itself. The only matter of importance is to know upon what altar we shall make this sacrifice. Those who offer it on the altar of that blind divinity, "the nature of things," remain still unconsoled. Those who, with Jesus, make it in the arms of the Heavenly Father, accomplish it with strength and joy. From the awakening of consciousness to its highest point of development, man carries within him this radical contradiction: he feels that there is a mortal conflict between the idea that he gradually forms of the world and the idea he forms of himself. The ego wishes to conquer and does actually conquer the world; it even goes beyond it by thought; but the world has its revenge; it dominates the ego, it crushes it beneath the weight of its invincible laws, and it swallows it up,—itself, its efforts, its works, its thought,—like an ephemeral nonentity. Jesus felt this opposition; He suffered from this conflict. He resolved the antithesis by a third term, in which was realised the other two: the notion of the Father, whose beneficent will is equally sovereign in man and in the universe. And it is this happy solution of the enigma of life that still renders the religion of Jesus the religion of hope.

Amongst men, in the midst of society, Jesus felt other relations and new obligations formed in His heart. His filial piety became a fraternal piety. The first commandment, "Thou shalt love the Lord thy God with all thine heart," necessarily gave birth to the second: "And thy neighbour as thyself." The Father who lives in me lives equally in my neighbour; He loves him as much as He loves me. I ought therefore to love Him in my neighbour as well as in myself. This paternal presence of God in all human souls creates in them not only a link but a substantial and moral unity which makes them members of one body, whatever may be the external and contingent differences which separate them. From the Fatherhood in heaven flows the brotherhood on earth. From a relation of righteousness and love towards God springs a similar relation between men.

In thus defining the religious connection of

Jesus with His brethren I am afraid of weakening it. For Him it was not a matter of theory; for He never constructed any theory or formulated any doctrine of human fraternity; it was with Him a passionate sentiment, a deep-felt solidarity and kinship, a true family life, in which this Elder Brother's heart reverberated on the one hand with the love and pity of the Father, and, on the other, with the miseries and distresses of His brethren. In His parables Jesus does not say "The Father" simply; He habitually says "the father of the family," "the head of the house." It is because the father does not exist without his children, and because humanity, on earth at least, is the family, by means of which the paternity of God is realised.

But in the society of men Jesus encountered sin with all its effects in the shape of moral deformity and physical suffering. From the contact of His filial piety with this enormous human misery sprang a twofold appeal: the voice of His Father in His soul, the plaint of His brethren all around; and to this double cry the answer was— His ministry of relief, of consolation, and salvation: "The Spirit of the Lord is upon Me, because He hath anointed Me to preach good tidings to the poor; He hath sent Me to proclaim release to the captives, and recovering of sight to the blind, to set at liberty them that are bruised, to proclaim the acceptable year of the Lord" (Luke iv. 18, 19, R.V.).

It all flows from the same source. It was not only individuals who needed to be healed and saved. The family of God was not less broken down, oppressed, disorganised, by all the powers of evil, a prey to hatred, selfish ambition, intestine wars. Would it not be necessary here also to effect a work of restoration, to reconstruct this family so highly-favoured of the Father for the salvation of the world, to inaugurate the kingdom of God announced by so many of the prophets, and expected so impatiently by all pious souls and all the victims of unrighteousness? This was His messianic vocation. But how would this victory of the Messiah be realised? Would it be the work of Divine power, flashing forth and executing its pitiless reprisals? Since the paternal heart of God had been opened and poured into His own, Jesus had perceived another law and another force, the law and force of love, which triumphs by self-sacrifice. Soon there arose in His consciousness a new image of the Messiah, that of the Servant of Jehovah, bearing the sins and miseries of His people, bruised, humiliated, dying to procure them life and healing. It was the gospel of the Cross. The further He advanced in this emptying of self, and in this work of love and pain, the larger and more luminous became the revelation of the Father in His soul. When at last He had the clear and perfect consciousness that He had no longer any will to do but the will of God, no other plan to follow than His mysterious designs, no other cause to serve and to defend but His, He did not doubt the final victory; His faith shone forth triumphantly, appropriating to itself, to express itself in perfect freedom, the boldest promises of the Ancient Testament and of the contemporary apocalyptic seers. By His union with the Father, the heir of the past felt Himself master of the future. On the throne of immolated love He has founded a kingdom that will never end. Such is the inner secret of His hope, such the moral and religious meaning of His prophecies of speedy victory, and of His return upon the clouds of heaven.

Jesus was fond of saying that a wise man knew how to bring forth from the treasury of his heart things new and old. It was in this way that He accomplished the most radical of religious revolutions while seeming only to fulfil the law and the prophets. What was there then that was so new and potent in the least of His discourses? The treasure of His filial consciousness. The inner inspiration springing up in them incessantly gives to every detail of His teaching, the oldest words, the most familiar metaphors, a meaning altogether new, a reach and bearing infinite. His speech confines itself to the antithesis that had become traditional with all the prophets, of man's weakness and God's strength, of sin and pardon, of repentance and confidence, of sickness and healing, of humility and exaltation. But He had a way of looking at them, and even of making them spring out of each other, that entirely renovated them. "Blessed are the poor in spirit, for theirs is the kingdom of heaven! Blessed are they that mourn, for they shall be comforted! Blessed are they that hunger and thirst after righteousness, for they shall be filled!" To press thus and to stimulate the sense of need, of misery and sin, so far that it changes into its opposite; to draw riches out of poverty, comfort out of sorrow, victorious strength from weakness; to find in sorrow for sin the germ of saintly life and in hunger and thirst the very source of satisfaction; to make every human soul thus pass through this inward drama of repentance and conversion in which it is regenerated and renewed,—such is the unique but admirable and all potent mystery of the Gospel.

Christ did not construct a theory of man, of his moral life, any more than He constructed a theory with respect to God and the universe. He was content to place Himself at the centre of the human consciousness, and to dig down to the source of life. He takes man as he is in all climates and in all conditions. He does not declare him to be radically impotent for good, but neither does He flatter him by veiling his natural misery. He knows him to be ardent and feeble, full of needs and of illusions, capable of conversion, subject to all passions, the victim of all slaveries. He treats him as diseased, which is the truth, and He does not think He can make him find the principle of a serious cure, save in the very sense of his malady. So far from blunting the edge of the moral law, He sharpens it as one sharpens a dissecting knife in order the better to pierce the living flesh and penetrate to the very joints and marrow; He infinitely enhances the demands of the traditional ideal; from the outward act He descends to the inward feeling; He makes lust equal to adultery, and anger or hatred to murder itself. He tells His disciples to love their enemies, to pray for those who persecute them, to answer violence by gentleness, and injuries by love. He speaks thus not to weaken the vigour of righteousness, but because He sees in love and gentleness a higher righteousness and the sole means of securing the final triumph of good over evil. That is why the righteousness of His friends exceeds the righteousness of the Scribes and Pharisees. It is no longer dictated by an outward letter, but it has, for soul, the very spirit of the Father, and, for inward rule, the ideal the Master has lit up in the conscience: "Be ye perfect, even as your Father in heaven is perfect."

This morality would easily become ascetic and appear impossible if it were not blended with an opposite element which renders it human and fruitful without either lowering or destroying it. That element is mercy and forgiveness; it is pure, unconditional grace which in misery makes room for hope, and in repentance opens the door to faith and to the work of faith. These two elements, inexorable law and unconditional grace, are so intimately blended in the Gospel of Christ that the Gospel only subsists in its originality and with its power by their perfect fusion and reciprocal and constant action. Without the inflexible rigours of the moral ideal, repentance would not be possible—at least it would never be profound enough to produce the renovation of the heart; but, without faith in the divine mercy, repentance itself, changing into despair, would be barren and ineffectual. These two elements of the Christian life are as fruitful by their union as they are impotent and liable to degeneration when isolated or opposed. What does Christian law become without the sentiment of love, without the impulse of mercy, but a sort of moral Stoicism, rigid and severe? And what would be the doctrine of grace apart from the sacred obligation of the law but the theory of a mischievous indulgence or a Pagan mysticism? To decompose the Gospel salt is to destroy its savour.

. . . .

4. *A Necessary Distinction*

At the close of this long meditation, one thing seems to me very clear, the necessity, or rather the obligation under which I stand henceforth of distinguishing between the purely moral essence of Christianity and all its historical expressions or realisations, even the highest and most faithful of them. If religion is an inward life, a real and felt relation between God and man, and if Christianity is that life carried to a higher degree, it is certain that religion in general, and Christianity in particular, must have the two characteristics of all living things. Life is a force, ideal in its essence, real in its manifestations. It can only manifest itself in the organisms that it creates and animates. But, while incarnating itself in its works, it does not exhaust itself or remain imprisoned in any of them. Jesus was well aware of this when He compared His gospel to the leaven which raises the dough and to the seed which germinates in the soil into which it falls.

This necessary distinction will neither be made nor admitted by everybody. Many who concede it in theory deny it in practice. Protestants smile at the Catholics, who identify Christianity with the Church. But while admitting and making the distinction, when it comes to particular churches and particular systems of dogmas, they resist and protest in their turn, if it becomes necessary to apply it to the Bible, and to distinguish between the Word and its human and historical expression.

Should we go further still? May we, ought we in all fidelity to apply the distinction to the Gospel of Christ itself and to the primitive form in which it has come down to us? Most of those who have accompanied us thus far will now recoil and leave us. They will employ against us the very same arguments which appear to them so pitiful when used with respect to the Church and to the Bible. For my part, I cannot comprehend this fear of the freedom left to criticism. It seems to me impossible to deny that in the teaching of Jesus there are parts which are uncertain, things which have been either badly understood or badly reported, an oriental and contingent form which needs to be translated into our modern languages. Who does not see that neither in His language nor in His thought is there anything absolute? Both of them are constantly determined by the generally received ideas of His time, the state of mind of His interlocutors; and unless you desire to deny that Jesus was a man of His age and of His race, how can you abstract Him from His environment and attribute to Him ideas which have neither date nor place? I have already compared Christianity to an oak which has lived and grown for eighteen centuries, and the Gospel to the acorn from which it sprang. But in that acorn itself, as in the tree, it is manifest that there are two things: a principle of life, and some matter borrowed from the Hebraic soil, with which the creating principle was obliged to amalgamate itself in order to enter into history and to become fruitful. The characteristic of life is to render possible and to institute the constant exchange of the materials with which it builds up its works. When this exchange has ceased, life has disappeared. If the Gospel of Jesus were something fixed and finished like a code of laws or a collection of formulas, it would no longer be a power of life. His words defy the centuries and never wither; they are truly eternal, because they leave free and do not imprison in a rigid and immutable letter the spirit of life which animates them.

Arrived at this point of view, I see the relations between Christianity and historical criticism change completely, and find myself once more in the greatest religious security. Criticism will always be a just cause of alarm to those who elevate any historical and contingent form whatever into the absolute, for the excellent reason that an historical phenomenon, being always conditioned, can never have the characteristics of the absolute. But criticism can do nothing against the Christian principle, which, brought back to the consciousness, always disengages itself from the relative and fleeting expressions in which it has clothed itself by the way. Criticism makes it to appear again in its ideal purity and eternal worth. Far from being injurious, it becomes necessary to it. It is not doubtful that the teaching and the work of Christ, having been preserved in the simple oral tradition for half a century, have not been transmitted to us without some corruptions and some legendary elements. What then does historical criticism, with all its rigour, do? Nothing but purify this uncertain tradition, remove the veils, set forth more certainly the authentic soul of Christ, and, consequently, place the Christian principle in its surest, clearest light.

What has been said of the Master's teaching is still more true of that of His disciples. The Christian plants have all sprung from the same seed; but they vary according to the soil in which they grow. They are all of the same species, but in that species there are innumerable varieties. How could the external result possibly have been the same whether the divine seed fell into the heart of a simple fisherman of Galilee, or a rabbi of genius, or a thinker brought up in the school of Alexandria? Could you possibly have the same Church, the same theology, the same ritual in Arabia and in Greece, among a savage race and in the university circles of Germany, at Rome or in England, in the Middle Ages in a feudal society, and in our democracies in a time of emancipated reason and free government?

And here it will be convenient to pause and reflect a moment on that wonderful variety in the historical forms of Christianity, none of which are perfect and none contemptible. A superficial examination may draw from this spectacle a lesson of indifference; a more conscientious and attentive study finds in it an opposite lesson, the lesson of an ever-pressing obligation on both individuals and churches never to repose in a deceitful satisfaction, but to progress unceasingly; for Christianity is nothing if it is not in us at once an ideal which is never reached and an inner force which ever urges us beyond ourselves.

5. *The Corruptions of the Christian Principle*

The differences which separate the historical forms of Christianity are, like those of religion in general, of two kinds: there are differences of kind and differences of degree. The differences of kind are those which arise from diversity of races, languages, civilisations, temperaments, genius. The differences of degree are those connected with the very intensity and purity of the Christian faith and life. Churches and peoples are diversified at once by their constitution and by their degree of culture and of moral life. It goes without saying that these two classes of differences are not juxtaposed; they are mixed incessantly and complicated endlessly. It remains none the less true that they provoke and legitimate two sorts of judgment. The first are accepted with tolerance and sympathy, since it would not be reasonable to blame a man for the colour of his skin. But the second may and should be discussed and analysed, for they imply intellectual errors or moral defects, the corruption or the weakness of the Christian principle, and they can only be corrected and remedied by discussion and criticism.

The Christian seed is never sown in a neutral and empty soil. No soul, no social state, is a *tabula rasa*. The place is always occupied by anterior traditions of ideas, rites, or customs, by institutions in possession. Christianity cannot therefore root itself anywhere without entering into conflict with the regnant powers, without giving battle to prejudices, manners, and superstitions which naturally resist, and which, when conquered, spring up again in other forms in the victorious religion. Take the Ebionite Christianity of the first centuries: what is it but a mixture, a compromise between Jewish and Christian elements? What shall we say of the Catholic Church after Constantine? Is it not true that, in the religious transformation at that time effected, there was a double and mutual conversion, and that it is hard to say whether the pagan world was more modified by Christianity or Christianity more deeply penetrated and invaded by the manners and the religion that it was supposed to replace?

In this order the most striking victories are never complete. Even after the most radical conversion, the old man survives, at least by its roots, in the new man. The Pharisee long survived in St. Paul after he became an Apostle of Christ. The same in human societies: political or moral revolutions never abolish the past. After those great battles in which passions and interests have often as much weight as noble ideas and generous sentiments, there is always established a sort of equilibrium by mutual concessions and spontaneous alliances between the vanquished and the victorious tendencies. Hence come what we have named the corruptions of the Christian principle in the course of historical Christianity, for which alone should be reserved the name of heresies.

It must not be imagined, however, that these

corruptions or heresies, against which it is the duty of Christian criticism ceaselessly to protest, are arbitrary things, or that their number is unlimited. On the contrary, they fall, and must necessarily fall, into two categories. The cause of the corruptions of the Christian principle in social life can only be found in the previous tradition, in one of the moral and religious tendencies that Christianity aspires to conquer and replace. Now, these tendencies may be reduced to two: the tendencies of the religions of Nature, or Pagan; and the tendency of the legal, or Jewish, religion. Closely examine all that has disfigured or that still disfigures historical Christianity, and you will see that each of these corruptions is connected, by its character, with a Jewish or a Pagan root. The Gospel as the religion of free spirit and pure morality has never had, and could never have had, any other enemies than Judaism or Paganism, ever ready to spring up in its bosom and transform it either into the religion of Nature or into the religion of the Law.

Christianity, for example, in its pure essence, implies the absoluteness of God—that is to say, His perfect spirituality and His perfect independence. Hence, worship in spirit and in truth, the only worship that can be universal, the only one that corresponds to the Christian idea of God. Therefore every tendency, even in Christianity itself, to shut up God in a phenomenal form, to bind Him to something material, local, or temporary, to blend the Creator with the creature, or to fill up the gap between them by a hierarchy of divine beings which, under pretext of serving us as intermediaries, interrupt our free and immediate communion with the Father, is, properly speaking, a resurrection of Paganism, and a return to idolatry. Paganism and idolatry, of which we pretend to have so much horror, are simply the localisation and materialisation, more or less conscious, of the divine spirit and of divine grace, whatever may be the visible organ to which you bind them, or on which you make their action to depend,—Pope of Rome or Pythoness of Delphi, images of gods or images of virgin and of saints, sacramental liturgies, the deification of a church, a priesthood, or a book.

Take another example: Christianity is not only the liberty of God; it is also His holiness; it is pure morality placed above all the instincts of nature; it is, finally, the unity of morality and religion. Hence, all that tends to break this unity, every blow at the divine law, every attempt to cultivate religious emotion apart from conscience, all magic and mystagogy, æsthetic piety, religious romanticism, Christianity à la Chateaubriand, sensuous mysticism,— these essays, so numerous in our day, at philosophic or at literary gnosis, these new religions without repentance or conversion, all these cults without any element of moral sanctification—these are so many corruptions of the Christian principle, and consequences more or less immediate of the Paganism always latent in the human heart.

By the side of this Pagan is the Judaising heresy. Christianity is not only moral law and intransigeant holiness; it is also unconditional love, grace, mercy, the inward action of the Spirit of God in the spirit of man in order to produce in it that which He desires to find, and to realise that which His law commands; it is everything that scandalised Pharisaism in the teaching and conduct of Jesus in regard to the sinful and the lost: pardon without reproach, rehabilitation and salvation through repentance and affection, the sincere impulse of the heart that has been raised above external works; the very opposite of legal compacts, meritorious and atoning virtue, formalist religion and ritual piety. All that tends to separate the Father from the child; that places the liberty and virtue of man outside and apart from God as having some merit in His sight ; all Pelagianism, every theory of salvation by works, every condition laid down to divine grace except faith to receive it: adhesion to a doctrinal formula, sacramental usages, priestly absolution, outward mortification, asceticism whether monkish or puritanical, which divides morality and, in the name of a fantastic sanctity, introduces dualism into the work of God,—all this should be called by its right name ; it should be taken for what it really is—a relapse into the legal and formalist spirit of Jewish Pharisaism.

Finally, I see on what condition Christianity may remain faithful to itself while realising itself in history. It is only by an incessant struggle of the Christian principle against all the elements of the past which find, alas, in human propensities, and in the inertia of the multitude, a complicity so constant and effectual. So far from religious indifference being permissible, critical action and Christian prayer become, in every church and every life, permanent duties. I now understand the paradox of Christ: "I am not come to send peace on the earth, but a sword." For the Christian principle, in fact, war is life. To cease to fight is to succumb ; it is to allow yourself to be submerged by the rising tide of human superstitions; it is to die. Who does not see the danger of allowing Christianity to become absorbed in one church form, Christian truth in one formula, the Christian principle in one of its particular realisations? All these contingent expressions, being imperfect, must be reformed sooner or later. How can they be unless the spirit of Christianity disengages itself without ceasing and floats above them as an ideal? For eighteen centuries a river of life has flowed through human history. Break down the barriers which fanaticism and superstition are always setting up athwart its course. If the waters cease to flow they stagnate, and corrupt and poison the very land it was their mission to fertilise.

CHAPTER III

THE GREAT HISTORICAL FORMS OF CHRISTIANITY

1. *The Evolution of the Christian Principle*

THE distinction between the Christian principle and its successive realisations renders it easy to resolve the question, formerly so much debated, as to the perfectibility of Christianity. It is perfect piety, plenary union with God, consequently the absolute and definitive Religion. But, regarded in its historical evolution, not only is it perfectible, but it must ceaselessly progress, since, for it, to progress is to realise itself. The germ could not be perfected in its essence, as germ and ideal type of the tree that it potentially contains. But the tree itself only comes into existence by the development of the germ. No reform, no progress, no perfecting, could raise Christianity above itself—that is to say, above its principle; for these reforms and this progress only bring it into closer conformity with that principle—that is, make it more Christian. On the other hand, the principle itself must enter into evolution in history in order to manifest its originality and its force, to realise in individual and social life, in the realm of thought and in the realm of action, in a word in the whole of civilisation, all its virtualities and all its consequences. Jesus saw this when He spoke the Parable of the Mustard Seed (Matt. xiii. 31-32).

This distinction has another advantage. It alone permits the Christian thinker to be equitable in his judgments in regard to all religious forms, to place himself at a truly historical point of view, and to reconcile, without weakness and without violence, what is due to truth and what to charity. Every sincere endeavour to express or to realise Christianity in a system or in a church becomes respectable so soon as you know how to discover in it, under formulas however strange and practices however gross, some effects of the Christian principle or some signs of its presence. If disdain and contempt are not permissible with regard to any type of Christianity however different from our own, neither is illusion to be tolerated with regard to our own church or to our personal piety. Perfection is nowhere to be found. Each community may repeat, and the larger, older, and more numerous it becomes the more will it need to repeat, the words of the Apostle Paul: "Brethren, I count not myself to have apprehended," etc. (Phil. iii. 13, 14). The habit we have got into of putting all the truth on our side and all error on the side of others, of thus opposing light and darkness, not only falsifies the judgment; it sours the heart and poisons piety; it dries up the feeling of fraternity, and is the perpetual sign of individual or collective vanity. Let each examine himself, let him judge his church without complacence in the light and spirit of Christ; he will soon attain to more humility and truth. He will never identify any particular church or its dogma with Christianity itself. However pure its teaching, however generous its deeds, he will reckon that this is, after all, but a commencement of Christianity, a mere nothing compared with what the Christian principle should have accomplished in the world in eighteen centuries.

Such is the feeling with which we should approach the history of Christianity. The field is vast; the vegetation in it is infinite; we must content ourselves with incompleteness. Being neither able nor desirous to say everything, I have been obliged to seek a commanding point of view from which it would be possible to take in that history in its entirety, and to take a bird's-eye view of the course it has followed. Faithful to this idea, namely, that the Christian principle is like leaven or a seed thrown into a gross, heavy mass of anterior traditions which it was meant gradually to raise and to transform, it is this struggle and this progress that I desire especially to describe. I shall endeavour to show how Christianity, always borrowing its forms from the environment in which it realises itself, after enduring them for a time, subsequently frees itself from and triumphs over the inferior and temporary elements which fetter it, and manifests from age to age a greater independence and a purer and higher spirituality. This progress is slow, obscure, oft interrupted, hindered by reactions or by moments of arrest; none the less striking, however, does it appear when, rising above these secondary complications, one measures the distance between the points of departure and arrival. Not only has Christianity never been better understood than in our own day, but never were civilisation or the soul of humanity taken in their entirety more fundamentally Christian.

When one follows the history of Christianity

from this higher point of view, one sees that it has passed through three very distinct phases and assumed three essentially different forms: the Jewish or Messianic, the Graeco-Roman or Catholic, the Protestant or modern, form. Let us see how it has passed from the one to the other.

2. *Jewish, or Messianic Christianity*

The first of these periods is usually omitted or suppressed. Being unable to admit that Catholicism is not the work of Christ and the apostles, or that the Church has varied its dogma or its institutions, Catholic theologians naively imagine that the first Christian communities of Jerusalem and Antioch resembled those of Rome, Milan, and Lyons in the fourth century; that Peter was the first of the popes and exercised for five-and-twenty years the supreme pontificate; that the apostles appointed bishops everywhere as their successors and the heirs of their power. In this way the history of Christianity became, in the Catholic tradition, a tissue of legends.

The theologians of Protestantism arrived by another road at an analagous conclusion. Under the influence of the dogma of the verbal inspiration of the New Testament, they were led to make of apostolic Christianity an ideal and abstract type which all the ages ought to force themselves to imitate and reproduce. And, as they profess to have returned to this type both in regard to ideas and to institutions and morals, they have made of this apostolic period the first chapter of the history of Protestantism, just as the Catholics have made of it the first chapter of the history of Catholicism. In both cases, it loses all distinct physiognomy and all reality.

By dissipating these prejudices, historical criticism has completely resuscitated that first form of Christianity. It is no longer possible to confound it with any other. It had its contrasts, its passions, its storms. Neither Jesus nor the apostles lived in the ideal or in paradisiacal peace. They quarrelled and were divided in the Church of Jerusalem as in our own. The subjects of the quarrels were different, but they did not consider them less grave than those which vex and trouble us. Peter, James, and Paul were not less divided in the first century over the question of circumcision and of the relations between Jews and Gentiles, than were Luther, Zwingle, and Calvin in the sixteenth over the doctrine of the Lord's Supper. From both camps, then as now, they sent forth pamphlets and anathemas. There were two opposite parties. There were the stubborn holders of tradition and its authority, and there were the innovators, or the partisans, sometimes as rash as they, of liberty of faith and individual inspiration ; and between the two there were the men of conciliation and the golden mean who were preoccupied especially in preventing schisms and arranging truces and treaties of peace, to be followed in their turn by new crises and fresh storms.

In this first form of Christianity, as in all that have followed it, there was a certain dualism, a mixture of heterogeneous and soon hostile elements. The struggle was bound to arise between the Christian principle and Jewish tradition. The new seed sown in that ancient soil could not germinate without rising in it and in places breaking up the thick hard crust. In the books of the New Testament that have preserved to us the picture of that first and powerful germination, side by side with the principle to which belongs the future we necessarily find old things which are on the way to death. It will be seen what an error they commit and what a wrong they do themselves who, misconceiving this historical complexity, sanctify and deify both these opposite elements, and place on the same level the eternally fruitful grain, and the chaff to-day dried up and utterly inert, a mere remnant of the Jewish stalk that bore it.

Conceived in this religious matrix of Judaism, the Christian principle, if I may so speak, could only take in it a body essentially Jewish in structure, substance, colour. I only speak, of course, of the body of this primitive Christianity, not of its soul, which, as I have shown, was altogether new. Now, its body was Jewish on two sides and in two aspects: by the persistence of the authority of the Law of Moses, and the practical observance of its precepts, from which the disciples of Jesus did not dream of detaching themselves; and, secondly, by the apocalyptic Messianism which dominated Jewish thought from the time of the Maccabees, and with which the first Christians were perhaps more imbued and more possessed than all the rest of their people.

Faith in the evangel of Jesus, full and joyful communion with the Father, habits of Jewish devotion, Messianic hopes,—all this formed, in the consciousness of the first disciples, a mixture of various elements and of things of very unequal value. These elements, in gradually revealing their disparate nature, could not fail to enter into contradiction and to engender conflicts in the very heart of apostolic Christianity. It was these contradictions and conflicts which set Christian thought in movement, and produced the life and progress of that early age, so that one may always rightly consider it as a creative and classic epoch, and hold it up as a normal example to the churches of all time; on condition, however, that it be not considered as an immutable mass of eternal verities, but taken in its natural movement, in its constant effort of progressive enfranchisement with regard to the past, in its heroic ascent towards religious forms and ideas, freer, more human, more conformed to the universal character, to the spirituality, and to the pure morality of the religion of Jesus.

"What, then," it will be said, "did not the Christ set His disciples free at the outset from all the errors and superstitions of the past? Did He not at once give them perfect dogmas, a completed form of worship, an immutable and completed system of ethics?" No; Jesus did nothing of the kind. So far from formally and systematically criticising the traditional religion of His people, so far from making *ex cathedra* that selection which the vulgar looked for, Jesus expressly refused it, as a method essentially false and irreligious. He did not wish to abolish anything by mere authority; He preferred rather to confirm the tradition in its totality, of which He was the heir and not the executioner. "Think not that I am come to destroy the Law or the Prophets: I am not come to destroy, but to fulfil" (Matt. v. 17).

His method was quite different. It was the method of the sower to whom He loved to compare Himself. In the furrow made by His word in the ancient soil of Judaism, He quietly and gently deposited new germs. In the traditional and theocratic notions of His race He placed contents altogether different drawn from His own religious experience, and from the sense of His filial relation to the Father. He then left time to do its work, to develop one after another the consequences of the principles He had planted in human souls. He sowed, and He and others reap from age to age the harvest He has sown.

Consider His attitude towards the Law of Moses. Not a jot or tittle of it is to fail or be neglected. He strengthens it rather than relaxes its claims; He deepens it, carries it inward, makes it infinitely more spiritual and searching. He gathers it up into two great commandments, and constrains the Law itself, if I may so speak, to surpass itself and transform itself into pure evangelical morality. That is what He meant by declaring that His work would be the fulfilment of the Law. Nothing was less violent; but nothing, at bottom, was more revolutionary. . . .

It is easy now to see the consequences of this method; history has revealed them. But those who heard the words of Jesus could not perceive these consequences. They had no idea probably that the day would come when to be faithful to the Master they would be obliged to break with Moses. They did not suddenly break with Judaism. Indeed, they had found in their new faith new motives for fervour and exactitude in their Mosaic piety. The first Christians in Jerusalem were honoured of all the people because of their assiduity in the Temple worship and for their exemplary devotion. They are therefore not enfranchised yet; they will have to free themselves from Judaism in the school of events into which they will be led by the Spirit of Jesus that is with them and dwells in them. The Christian principle will have to reconquer its independence of the Judaism which dominates and hems them in on every side. This will be the work of more than a century of conflict and controversy. All Christians will not enter into the movement with the same decision ; they will not march abreast on the path of liberty. Many will be stupid and turn back. Progress would not have been made if the Divine Spirit that had raised up Jesus had not raised up valiant men like Stephen, Saul of Tarsus, Barnabas, the author of the Epistle to the Hebrews, and that of the Fourth Gospel, to carry on the struggle against the bondage of Judaism and carry it to complete victory. When you pass from the one to the other, from the discourse of Stephen to the Epistle to the Galatians, from the Epistle to the Romans to the Johannean theology, you clearly see the march of progress. At the end of the first century Christianity is so independent of national and traditional Judaism that the one treats the other, without any further scruple, as an alien and hostile religion.

More adhesive still to the Christian principle, less easy to strip off, was the second Jewish wrappage, apocalyptic Messianism. Jesus had so thoroughly consecrated it by calling Himself the Messiah and by inaugurating the kingdom of God, that His Gospel might be named a "Christian Messianism." In His discourses He seems to have confirmed it still more expressly than the Law of Moses. No doubt He proceeded in both cases alike. In all the theocratic notions which constituted this popular Messianism, He lodged a new content, a religious and moral element which must, in the long run, make them burst their trammels and elevate Messianism above itself. But He did not bring to it any negative and abstract criticism, any more than He did to the divers parts of the Mosaic tradition; He never said either that it must be abandoned or that it must be retained; He deposited in it the new principle; but He left in it many obscurities, abandoning to time and to the force of things the care of drawing forth the consequences and clearing up confusions.

For His own part He wished simply to maintain intact beneath these apocalyptic forms the principle and the inspiration of His inward piety. It was in accordance with these that He interpreted the popular beliefs, adapting them with a perfect sovereignty to the moral aim and nature of His work. As with the Mosaic Law, so with Messianism; He is its Master, not its slave. He uses it, but does not abandon Himself to it. These hopes never trouble the clearness of His religious vision; they do not take away His self-possession, or alter the direction, always exclusively moral, of His acts. He accepts the title of Messiah, but only after substituting the idea of the suffering and humiliated for the national and triumphant

Messiah. If He preaches the kingdom of God, He takes care to explain the conditions and the true goods of the kingdom—humility, repentance, childlike confidence, righteousness, disinterested love, the joy of serving God and man. He leaves to men of the flesh the pomp and splendour which dazzle the eyes of the flesh. He admires the grandeur of John the Baptist more than that of Herod. The kingdom of God will not come with ostentation. It will begin like an unseen seed that a man puts into the ground.

At the outset of His work Jesus encountered a mysterious temptation. This was the conflict of His consciousness with the seductions of the popular Messianism. He triumphed over it with difficulty; but thenceforth He was always on His guard in that direction. Is it not remarkable that this very temptation returned to Him through the mouth of Peter? Jesus treats as Satan the first of His apostles, and refers to the devil in person and the prince of darkness suggestions of this nature which tend to make Him deviate from the road marked out by the inspiration of His heart. He avoids the title Messiah until the day when He is able to join with it the image of the Cross. He disdains the title, "Son of David," preferring to all others that of "Son of Man," a title that was not open to the same mistakes. On this road of renunciation He must sacrifice not only His ease, His joys, and His repose, but also, at each step, some of the beliefs of Israel, and some of the glories of the Messiah. He never hesitates. His people reject Him, and He turns to His Father and says to Him: "Even so, Father, for so it seemed good in Thy sight." He agonises in Gethsemane, the Messiah agonises in Him, and He prays thus: "Father, not My will, but Thine be done."

Hence comes His freedom of spirit, the elevation of His view in the interpretation of events, as also His pious and trustful reserve in face of the enigmas and obscurities that His glance cannot penetrate. John the Baptist is beheaded in prison: singular destiny for that formidable Elijah who was to inaugurate by thunder and lightning the Messianic era, the dream of all patriots! Is Jesus offended by it? Does He hesitate to declare that John at that very moment is "the Elias which was for to come"? What a defiance to the oracles of the popular Messianism! When the sons of Zebedee desire Him to reserve for them the foremost places in His future kingdom, He merely speaks to them of the baptism of martyrdom, and teaches them that they must leave such things at the disposal of the Father. No doubt, He never contradicts apocalyptic predictions; on the contrary He applies to Himself all the promises of glory and of triumph; but always in subjection to the Father's will. Asked as to the date of the Messiah's advent, He answers that He does not know, that they must observe the blossoms on the fig-tree and the signs of the times around Himself; that they must watch and pray, possess their souls in patience, and abandon to the Father the decisions of which He keeps the impenetrable secret.

I speak of freedom of interpretation and of pious reserve, not of hypocritical and sceptical accommodation. We cannot doubt that Jesus accepted at the outset, and shared, at bottom, the Messianic beliefs in which He had been trained like all the children of His race. That His disciples, in reporting His discourses on this point, exaggerated and materialised them, need not be denied. But, on the other hand you can hardly explain the unanimity of the earliest Christian tradition in expecting His return upon the clouds if Jesus had professed entirely opposite ideas. After all, is there anything more astonishing in His sharing on this matter the hopes of His time than in the fact of His having explained certain mysterious maladies as His contemporaries did by demoniacal possession, or of His attributing Psalm cx., as did certain of the rabbis, to King David; to the first Isaiah the work of the second, and to Moses the redaction of the Pentateuch? These current and traditional ideas, however, which came to Him, not from heaven, but from His race and His environment, never succeeded in corrupting the immutable purity of His inner piety or in falsifying the divine inspirations of His heart. Whenever there was contradiction between the Messianic beliefs or the Law of Moses, on the one hand, and the consciousness of Jesus, on the other, it was not the latter but the former that gave way and were transformed.

The disciples were not so free as the Master. Their faith remained a long time bound to these hopes of the future. Why had they left all and followed Him but because He had appeared to them to be the bearer and the depository of the divine promises? His death, which seemed to belie their beliefs, only served to give them another turn. They corrected prophecy. Instead of one Advent of the Messiah they imagined two, the first in humiliation, the second in glory. The one having been realised, they expected the other with a more ardent confidence. No one doubted it was near. The apostle Paul lived in this hope as well as the author of the *Apocalypse*, the compilers of the synoptic gospels, and the editors of " The Teaching of the Apostles." The time is short : the Master comes : *Maranatha.* This was the watchword of all the early Christians. This faith in the imminent return of Christ and of the end of the world dominates all the thoughts as well as the feelings of the apostles : it determines and colours their Christology, their theory of Redemption, their ethics, their idea of salvation, so that to expound their writings and estimate the worth of their reasonings, the historian must always read them and explain them in this light. It is for this reason that their Christianity merits the name of Messianic, and could not be, in this Jewish form, an absolute *norm* for all the ages.

The disciples of Jesus, however, found themselves in a school in which they could not perpetually mistake the lessons. The Christian principle had appeared to be at one with Messianism ; it was something altogether different and could not continue for ever to be mixed up with it. Under the contradiction of events and the action of the spirit of Jesus, they soon began to see the dawn of a process of spiritualisation in their apocalyptic beliefs. This progress is manifest in the letters of St. Paul when read in their order and with attention. In the first, he hopes before he dies to witness the advent of the Lord. But, from the Second Epistle to the Corinthians, the image of death and martyrdom begins to interpose itself between his faith and that glorious ideal, which evermore seems to recede into the future. It never entirely disappears, but this preoccupation with the return of Jesus diminishes and occupies a smaller space in his later epistles. On the contrary, the work of Jesus, considered in the past and in its redemptive efficacy, the Christian life conceived as a life of faith and love, as an imitation of Jesus Christ and an inheriting of His Spirit, receive ever-increasing developments. Insensibly, the centre of gravity of apostolic Christianity changes; from the hypnotising contemplation of the Messianic future, it passes to the sanctifying meditation on the passion of Christ, on His teaching, and redeeming work. This is best seen in the Epistle to the Hebrews, and in the Fourth Gospel, in which the Jewish Messiah is transformed into the eternal *Logos*, the light of all men here below, and the principle of the universal religion.

The work of emancipation that men alone could not accomplish, God Himself achieved. The conquests of the Church in the Empire, and especially the double and irreparable ruin of Jerusalem and the Jewish nation under Titus and under Hadrian, opened on the future other prospects. The world continued. It was necessary to settle down and live in it. Montanism was merely a last outburst of fever. By the end of the second century, Jewish Messianism was so nearly dead that its obstinate adherents were regarded as heretics by the Church at large. Organised into a hierarchy, the Church substituted itself resolutely for the ancient people of Israel, and represented itself as heir to the ancient promises. The advent of the kingdom of God becomes the advent and the victory of the Catholic Church over all the other powers of earth. The Messianic Theocracy is transformed into a Church Theocracy. Messianism gives place to Catholicism.

3. *Catholic Christianity*

Transplanted from the poor and arid soil of Hebraism into the rich and fruitful loam of Graeco-Roman civilisation, the Christian plant was sure to grow apace and be transformed. Catholicism is as much Pagan as Apostolic Messianism was Jewish—from the same causes, and according to the same law. More Greek in the East, more Roman in the West, it bears always and everywhere the traces of its origin. Study successively all the features of the Catholic Church, and you will find on each of them this indelible mark.

The dogmas of the Councils and the theology of the Fathers, who does not see at the first glance their true character? Who does not see that the material is Greek in form, in colour, in every fibre of its tissue? Whence came those terms and notions, of which Hebraism knew nothing, but which the theologians of all the schools will henceforth bandy to and fro—those abstract concepts, substance and hypostasis, nature and person, essence and accident, matter and form? Whence came the science of the Fathers of the Church, their exegesis, their history, their logic, their psychology, and that lofty metaphysic which has so completely transformed the Prophetic into a Platonic firmament? All this came from Athens, Ephesus, Samos, and Miletus, *viâ* Alexandria and Rome. The Justins, the Athenagorases, the Clements and the Basils, Athanasius even more than Arius, Jerome as well as Augustine, had been nourished from their childhood on Greek and Latin literature. They had read Plato Heraclitus, Zeno, Philo, Cicero, Posidonius, and

Seneca as much and more perhaps than the Old Testament. What is there astonishing in the fact that their theology should have followed step by step the theology of neo-Platonism until this latter, for Augustine, should have become the true introduction to the Gospel, and that in the Middle Ages the names of Plato and Aristotle should have been invested with an authority not less than those of Isaiah, St. Paul, and St. John?

Or shall we pass to the constitution of the Church? What is that but the exact counterpart of the constitution of the Roman Empire: the parish modelling itself on the municipality, the diocese on the province, the metropolitan regions on the great prefectures, and, at the top of the pyramid, the bishop of Rome and the papacy, whose ideal dream is simply, in the religious order, the universal and absolute monarchy of which the Cæsars had first set the pattern? Or would you consider the moral life and the type of piety? It is true that at the outset, and so long as the persecutions continued, there is a great contrast between Jewish or Christian morals and manners and those of Roman or Greek society. But, with time, the contrast is singularly attenuated. If the Church conquered the world, the world had its revenge within the Church. . . . What is that monkish asceticism imposing celibacy on the clergy, exalting virginity, multiplying pious works of merit, and replacing, by factitious and sterile duties, the duties dictated by nature and essential to society,—what are all these but survivals of a dualism and the imitation of an ideal which, come from the East, seduced the feverish imagination of an expiring world? The monks, the anchorites and their theology of impotent celibates, did they save Egypt, Syria, and Byzantium?

During this time, what did worship, adoration, religion, properly speaking, become? Between earth and heaven there reappeared the whole ancient hierarchy of gods and demi-gods, of heroes, nymphs, and goddesses, replaced by the Virgin Mother, angels, demons, saints. Each town, each parish, every fountain, had its patron or its patroness, its tutelary guardian, to whom they addressed themselves more familiarly than to God in order to obtain temporal blessings and the grace for every day. The saints have their specialities like the minor deities of former times. Some cured fevers, some diseases of the skin. This one had charge of travellers, that of harvests, a third of articles that had been lost, a fourth of needed heirs in families in danger of decay. With this mythology, all the superstitions were revived, down to the grossest fetichism: pilgrimages, chaplets, litanies, the veneration of images, signs of the cross, rites and sacraments conceived after the manner of the ancient mysteries. And all this is done with a sort of unconsciousness, very gradually, and as the effect of a zeal that was supposed to be Christian. The heads of the Church recommend missionaries not to destroy the temples of the false gods, but to consecrate them to the true one, and to replace their images by images of the saints, and the rites of the old cults by similar ceremonies. Names and etiquettes were thus changed, but not the things themselves. At Rome, beneath the basilica of St. Peter, a superb statue was erected to the Prince of the Apostles. This was formerly a statue of Jupiter. Its great toe has been worn down by the kisses of the faithful. Before Christianity, they kissed the foot of the master of the gods; now they kiss the foot of Peter. Is the cult of a different order and the devotion of a higher quality?

These, however, are but the forms of Catholicism; let us go deeper and try to reach its generating principle. This principle should be found in the central dogma of the Catholic system, that in it which commands and regulates all the parts, which constitutes its unity and strength. To designate this central dogma is not difficult. The catechism teaches us that it is the dogma of the Church, of its infallibility and traditional continuity, of its divine origin and supernatural powers. Protestants affirm that they belong to the Church because they belong to Christ. Catholics reverse the terms: no one is in communion with Christ, no one really belongs to Him, unless he belongs to the Church. Thus faith in the Church and submission to the Church are put into the forefront and remain the one thing needful and essential. One is a Catholic by the fact of his implicit acceptance of the sovereign authority of the Church; one ceases to be a Catholic when that submission ceases. From which it is easy to conclude that the principle of Catholicism is the realisation of the Christian principle—that is to say, of the reign of God and of Christ, in the form of a visible institution, an organised social body, an external power, exercising itself by means of that which is the very soul of the institution—a priesthood endowed with supernatural functions and attributes.

The immediate consequence of this first principle was the rupture of the organic union realised in the Gospel of Christ between the religious element and the moral element. Nothing is more striking in the Sermon on the Mount and in all the Parables of Jesus, nothing better attests the superiority of Christianity to anterior cults, nothing proves with greater force and clearness that it is the perfect and definitive Religion, than that mutual penetration, that fusion, that identification, in a word, of religion and morality, till then separate and often opposed to each other. The Christ did not desire in religion anything that was not in morality, or in morality anything that was not religious. Thus did He bring back piety from without, and made of it the inner inspiration which penetrates and transforms the whole life, a hidden flame, a ferment acting from the centre to the surface, the soul in the body, ever invisible and everywhere present. He thus founded the absolute autonomy of the religious and of the moral life which no longer are divided, but appear simply as the two sides of consciousness; the one interior and turned towards God, the other exterior and turned towards the world. In creating in us the sense of our sonship to God, Jesus did not admit the intervention of any external authority between the Father and the child. The universal priesthood, with which, by His spirit, He invests the least of His disciples, excludes in principle all supernatural priesthood. "Call no man master on earth, for one is your Master in heaven; and all ye are brethren." The children must have free access to the Father.

But, from the moment the Christian principle, instead of entering as divine inspiration into the consciousness, sets itself up as a visible institution in society, it is evident that this organic union is broken, and the autonomy of the individual consciousness compromised. The religious element affirms itself on its own account, and imposes itself from without on the mind of the faithful as a divine authority. The ancient dualism, which the Gospel surmounted, reappears in a profounder form; it brings in its train a universal supernaturalism—that is to say, a mechanical conception of the relations between God and the world. Instead of a penetration we have a superposition of two elements. The clergy separates itself from the laity and superposes itself upon it as the necessary intermediary between earth and heaven. Religious society, constituted under the form of a government, superposes itself upon the civil society that it desires to rule; grace superposes itself upon nature, acting on it from above in the sacraments; the morality of the Church, in so far as it is a supernatural morality, superposes itself upon the natural morality of conscience; revelation upon reason; divine dogmas upon human science; the spiritual power of the priest upon the temporal power of the family and of the State. Everywhere, within and without, the division breaks out, and you see arise in man and in society an intestine struggle which will never end; for these two original forces that it brings into conflict, religion and nature, are equally powerful and eternal.

Catholicism began, then, in the Church of the second century when, under the unconscious action of tradition and of pagan habits, the need was felt of objectivising and materialising the Christian principle in an external fact, of imprisoning the kingdom of God in a visible institution, the immanent revelation of the Holy Spirit in the decisions and acts of a priesthood. This tendency, once born, would be irresistible. Ideal and transcendent as it was at first, the Christian principle would become ever more external and political. Absorbing all Christianity, and holding in its hands all the graces of God, the Church would naturally present itself to the world as the permanent mediator and the grand magician. It was its part to effect the salvation of sinners, and, for this, it would need, like the ancient priests, to offer daily to God an agreeable oblation, an expiatory sacrifice of infinite value to atone for the infinite sins of the world. Thus the Church transformed the commemoration of the death of Christ into a *real* renewal of the sacrifice on Calvary; the Holy Supper became the mass; the fraternal table was turned into an altar; the elder or presbyter was changed into a priest and pontiff, and the bread of the communion into a divine victim. The dogma of transubstantiation was bound to follow; to the materialisation of Christianity in the Church corresponds the materialisation of God in the host.

By virtue of the same principle, Christian piety becomes devotion, *i.e.* a ritual and meritorious practice, as in the ancient cults. But we must not be unjust and attribute something to Catholicism that it condemns. It does not say that external practice is sufficient; the Church esteems it vain and even culpable unless accompanied by the affections and the will.

. . . . . .

The first and principal act of piety is submission to the Church. Its dogmas may be irrational, contradictory; its commandments may seem arbitrary, foreign to the natural conscience, sometimes in contradiction with it; no matter.

Reason, conscience, all must abdicate, and all submit. . . . In the Church, the Christian state must always be a state of minority, for the tutelage that it accepts will never cease. And the authority of the Church, being on this point sovereign and indefectible, could not remain invisible and indeterminate. An imperious logic pushed it from the first to incarnate itself in its organs, more and more apparent and simplified. First it was lodged in individual bishops, then in councils, until the Pope when speaking *ex cathedra* became the sole authority. In 1870 the Council of the Vatican, by promulgating the dogma of Papal infallibility, drew the irresistible conclusion from the premises laid down in previous centuries. The evolution of Catholicism was completed. The transformation of Christianity into a sacerdotal theocracy was achieved. The first is realised and exhausted in the second, and the distinction we established, when speaking of the essence of Christianity, between the Christian principle and its historical realisations, is not merely effaced; it no longer has any meaning.

From which follow two consequences which every day become more clear and patent. The first is that the Catholic Church, notwithstanding the desires of Leo XIII., is fatally condemned to be intolerant and intransigeant towards all others. The second is that it is contradictory to expect any reform in that Church, or even to speak of it ; for the Church could not admit the necessity of reform without renouncing all its pretentions. A river never turns back to its source. Catholicism can only exist by struggling for supremacy. It must be all or nothing.

At the same time, things are not so simple as our systems. The logic of ideas does not exhaust the reality of life. Behind abstract principles there are pious souls. . . . In Catholicism there has always been a latent Protestantism, by which I mean a protest, mute or spoken, direct or indirect, of the Christian principle against the oppressions of external and tyrannical authority. . . . Without the continuous presence of the Christian spirit in the Catholic Church, the Reformation would have been impossible. Without the triumph of the sacerdotal spirit it would have been unnecessary. Protestantism sprang out of Catholicism because it was virtually contained in it.

4. *Protestant Christianity*

It is strangely to mistake the nature of the Protestant Reformation of the sixteenth century to see in it a sort of semi-rationalism, the inconsistent exercise of free examination, or the revolutionary introduction of a foreign philosophical principle into the warp and woof of Christianity. You have only to read the biography of the Reformers and to make a slight analysis of their soul to form an entirely different idea of their work. The first and almost the only question which preoccupies and troubles them is an exclusively religious and practical question: "What must we do in order to be justified before God? How may we attain to peace of soul and to the assurance of pardon and of life eternal?" To find this peace, this pardon and salvation, which the Church could not procure for them, they determined to turn back and quench their thirst at the primitive sources of the Gospel. They went back to the original documents because they were persuaded that Christianity had been corrupted in the course of centuries; they wished to have it in its purity. Their whole reformation was to consist in this restoration of primitive truth.

But history never recommences. This return to the past and this re-reading of the Bible were accompanied by a religious experience and an act of consciousness which made of their enterprise something essentially new and original, and which rendered it immeasurably fruitful. It is unnecessary to seek elsewhere than in psychological experience the germ of Protestantism. It was in the humble cell of a convent at Erfurt and in the soul of a poor monk that the drama was first enacted from which sprang the revolution that has changed the face of the world.

Luther entered the convent with a faith in the authority of the Church and in the efficacy of its rites as serious and entire as that of any monk. "If it was possible," he said afterwards, "to reach Heaven by monkery, I was resolved to reach it by that road." For years he shrank from nothing that might render God propitious; he multiplied his acts of devotion and his works of penance. There is a striking analogy between the experiences of Luther under the monachal régime and those of Saul of Tarsus under the discipline of the Pharisaic Law. The *dénoûment* was the same. For the second time, the system of pious works was found powerless to appease a conscience which roused against itself the rigour of its own ideal. This struggle against an external law could only exasperate the sense of sin to the point of despair. Paul and Luther, in precisely the same manner, experienced the inward emptiness and radical worthlessness of the religious system in which they had been trained. The more they had tried to realise it in its perfection, the more had they found it wanting. Catholicism, considered as a means of salvation, was rejected by the religious and moral consciousness of Luther, before it was condemned by exegesis and by reasoning. To reach this sentence without appeal the Saxon monk had but to maintain inflexible the demands of the divine law and to measure, without illusion, the abyss that separated him from God, and that no human works could fill. It was in this way that he found himself shut up to the essence of the Gospel of Jesus Christ; he found the peace that fled from him in the pure and simple acceptance of the glad tidings of the paternal love of God, in the confidence that He gives gratuitously that which man can never conquer for himself, namely, the remission of sins and the certitude of eternal life. What then is faith? Is it still intellectual adhesion to dogmas or submission to an external authority? No. It is an act of confidence, the act of a childlike heart, which finds with joy the Father whom it knew not, and Whom, without presumption, it is happy henceforth to hold with both its hands. That is what Luther found in

Paul's great words: "The just shall live by faith." In this radical transformation of the notion of faith restored to its evangelical meaning is to be found the principle of the greatest religious revolution effected in the world since the preaching of Jesus.

Let us therefore here set forth the radical opposition between the Catholic principle and the Protestant principle in order that we may thoroughly understand the internecine war that was henceforth to be waged between them. In vain will eminent men in both camps, with the most generous and conciliatory intentions, arise and endeavour to find some middle ground, and effect a pacific reunion of the two halves of Christendom. All compromises, all diplomatic negotiations, will fail, because each of the two principles can only subsist by the negation of the other. Having attained to salvation, to full communion with God, independently of and in collision with the authority and the discipline of the sacerdotal Church, how could Luther recognise them any longer as divine and submit to them with sincerity and confidence? The ancient edifice had been the more thoroughly ruined, inasmuch as it had become useless and had been replaced. The originality of Luther consisted in this: his religious enfranchisement sprang from his own piety, and he founded his freedom on his sense of sonship, on the sense he had of his quality and titles as a child and heir of God. How could such a consciousness submit itself to the yoke again without denying itself? Catholicism, on the other hand, cannot be less intransigeant. To recognise in any degree whatever that it is possible to a Christian to enjoy pardon and the sense of the divine fatherhood apart from its dogmas and its priesthood, would not this be to abdicate all its pretensions, and to transform itself to the point of destruction?

No doubt, in actual life, this opposition is attenuated by the fact that in all Catholicism there is a latent Protestantism, and in all Protestantism a latent Catholicism. Between Port-Royal and Geneva, between Bossuet and Leibniz, between Leo XIII. and the Anglican Church, the distance seems but little. It is an illusion. Like two electricities of the same name, no sooner do they come into contact than they repel each other and separate more widely than before. In Catholicism Christianity tends to realise itself as a theocratic institution; it becomes an external law, a supernatural power, which, from without, imposes itself on individuals and on peoples. In Protestantism, on the contrary, Christianity is brought back from the exterior to the interior; it plants itself in the soul as a principle of subjective inspiration which, acting organically on individual and social life, transforms it and elevates it progressively without denaturalising and doing violence to it. Protestant subjectivity becomes spontaneity and liberty, just as necessarily as Catholic objectivity becomes supernaturalism and clerical tyranny. The religious element is no longer separated from the moral element; it no longer asserts itself as a truth or a morality superior to human truth and human morality. The intensity of the religious life is no longer measured by the number or the fervour of pious works or ritual practices, but by the sincerity and elevation of the life of the spirit. All asceticism is radically suppressed. Science is set free along with conscience; the political life of the peoples, as well as the inner life of the Christian. Man escapes from tutelage, and in all departments comes into possession of himself, into the full and free development of his being, into his majority.

This subjective character of a religion strictly moral stamps itself with energy on all the specific doctrines of Protestantism. It would be superfluous to dwell upon the doctrine of justification by faith; its subjective character is evident. No doubt the term justification has a legal colour and awakens the idea of a tribunal. But it must not be forgotten that this tribunal is nothing but the inner court where man and God meet each other face to face, where man is accused by his own conscience, and where the sentence which absolves him is the inward witness of the Holy Spirit, heard by him alone.

The doctrine of the sovereign authority of Scripture in matters of faith might seem at first sight to set up an external authority. And it is very true that certain Protestants have often understood it in the Catholic sense, and have employed it to exercise some violence on their own conscience or on the conscience of their brethren. But they never succeed for long; they soon fall into a too flagrant contradiction. The authority of the Bible is never separated in Protestantism from the right of the individual to interpret it freely, and from the personal duty of assimilating the truths he discovers in it. What therefore are those Protestants doing who attempt to set up a confession of faith as absolute and obligatory truth but imposing on their brethren their own subjective interpretation, and, consequently, denying to others the right which they exercise themselves? Nor let it be forgotten, on the other hand, that the obligation laid on each Christian to read the Bible and draw from it his faith is a perpetual and fruitful appeal to the energy of thought and to the autonomy of the inner life. The authority of Scripture, so far from being a menace to Christian liberty, is its invincible rampart. Not only has the Protestant Christian in the name of the Bible triumphed over eighteen centuries of tradition, but it is the Bible, an appeal to the Bible ever better understood, which has saved Protestant theology from scholasticism, which has prevented it from congealing in a confession of faith, and which, leaving the principle of the Gospel in an ideal transcendence in relation to all its historical expressions or realisations, has maintained, and still maintains, the spirit of reform in the Churches of the Reformation.

The doctrines of grace and of predestination, which are at the centre of Calvinism, have no other meaning. Souls religiously inert see in these doctrines nothing but an abuse of blind power, a sort of divine *fatum*, breaking every spring in the human soul. Nothing appears to be more oppressive or more immoral. But this is only an appearance. There is really no predestination for irreligious souls. This doctrine is but the expression of the inner basis of all true piety, which is nothing if it is not the sense, the feeling, of the presence and the sovereign and continuous action of God in each soul and in all the universe. No other sentiment gives so much spring and vigour to the human will, nothing raises it to such a height or makes it so invincible to all assaults from within and without. "If God be for us, who can be against us?" etc. (Rom. viii. 31-39). How is it that the Calvinistic Puritans of New England were the founders of modern liberty, and the Jesuits, those admirable theorisers on freewill, the precursors of all the servitudes? It is with predestination as it is with religion itself. Conceived as exterior to the life of the soul, it gives birth, no doubt, to a crushing despotism; conceived as an inward inspiration, sustaining the initiative and even the liberty of the individual, it becomes, in the Christian soul, the source of a force which nothing can break or subdue.

But the point at which the antithesis between Protestantism and Catholicism becomes most patent is the doctrine of the natural priesthood of all Christians as opposed to that of the supernatural priesthood of a privileged clergy. The free and perpetual communion of believing souls with the Father is the foundation of the independence of each and of the fraternal equality of all. The tap-root of clericalism is cut. The individual is a priest before the interior altar of his conscience; the father is a priest in his household; the citizen, if so he wills, in the city.

The Catholic notion of dogma vanishes with all the rest. To speak of an immutable and infallible dogma, in Protestantism, is nonsense; that is to say, if we accept the dictionary definition of dogma—the promulgation by the Church of an absolute formula. The decision of a Church cannot have more authority than that Church itself. Now, no Protestant Church holds itself, or can hold itself without denying itself, to be infallible. How then could it communicate to its definitions an infallibility that it did not itself possess? Protestant confessions of faith are always conditioned in time, and can never be definitive; they are always revisable, consequently they are always liable to criticism and to reform. Thus ceases the solidification of traditional dogma. The old ice melts beneath the breath of knowledge and of piety. The river takes again its natural course, and evolution, under the control of a perpetual criticism, becomes the law of religious thought, as of all other human activities.

From these observations and analyses (necessarily abridged) the true nature of Protestantism will have become sufficiently clear. It is not a dogma set up in the face of another dogma, a Church in competition with a rival Church, a purified Catholicism opposed to a traditional Catholicism. It is more and better than a doctrine, it is a method; more and better than a better Church, it is a new form of piety; it is a different spirit, creating a new world and inaugurating for religious souls a new régime. It is equally evident that Protestantism cannot be imprisoned in any definitive form. It leads to variety of formulas, rites, and associations as necessarily as the Catholic principle leads to unity. No limit can be set to its development. Always interior, invisible, ideal, the religious principle that it represents accompanies the life and activity of the spirit into all the paths that man may pursue and in all the progress he may make. Nothing human is alien to it; nor is it alien to anything that is human. It solves the problem of liberty and authority as it is solved by free and ordered governments; it does not suppress either of the terms, but conciliates them by reducing authority to its pedagogic *rôle*, and by making the Christian spirit the soul and inner rule of liberty.

By very reason of its superiority, and of the conditions of general culture that it presupposes, this form of Christianity could only appear after all the others. The spirit can only become self-conscious by distinguishing itself from the body in which at first it seems as if diffused, and by opposing to it an energetic moral protest. "That is not first which is spiritual, but that which is natural; and afterwards that which is spiritual" (1 Cor. xv. 46. Cf. Gal. iv. 1-5). This divine plan, which the apostle discovered in the ancient history of humanity, is repeated in the history of Christianity. The Messianic form corresponds to infancy, to that brief, happy age in which the impatient imagination nourishes itself on dreams and illusions which the experience of life soon dissipates without killing or even enfeebling the immortal hope at the heart of it. The Catholic form, which succeeds it, endures longer and corresponds to the age of adolescence, in which education is painfully prosecuted, and it demands a strict external discipline and masters whose authority must not be questioned or discussed. It was in this way that Catholic discipline and authority conducted the slow, laborious education of the pagan and barbarian world up to the sixteenth century.

But a moment must arrive when the work of education had succeeded, when the leading strings essential to childhood began to be a bondage and a hindrance. The pedagogic mission of the Church, like that of the family itself, had its limit and its term in the very function it fulfilled. That function was to make adult Christians and free men, not men without rule, but Christians having in themselves, in their conscience and their inner life, the supreme rule of their thought and conduct. This new age of autonomy, of firm possession of self, and of internal self-government, is that which Protestantism represents, and it could only commence in modern times—that is to say, with that general movement which, since the end of the Middle Ages, is leading humanity to an ever completer enfranchisement, and rendering it more universally and more individually responsible for its destinies.

It may be remarked that by this evolution, and under its Protestant form, the Christian principle was only returning to its pure essence and its primitive expression. It could only recognise itself, take cognisance of its true nature, separate itself from that which was not itself; it could only disencumber itself of every material, temporary, or local element, of all by which it had become surcharged in the course of ages, and which was neither religious nor moral, by remounting to its source, and by renewing its strength, through reflection and criticism, at its original springs. That is why Protestantism has taken the form of this return to the past, for in it Christianity does not surpass itself; it simply tries to know itself better and to become more faithful to its principle. In the consciousness of Christ, what did we find was the essence of the perfect and eternal piety? Nothing more than moral repentance, confidence in the love of the Father and the filial sense of His immediate, active presence in the heart: the indestructible foundation of our liberty, of our moral dignity, of our security, in face of the enigmas of the universe and the mysteries of death. Is it not to this eternal gospel that we must always return? To finish its course and complete its work, will humanity ever discover another viaticum that will better renew its courage and its hope?

5. Conclusion

Here I must stop. At the outset I spoke of a personal confession, and it seems to me as if it were nearly complete. In sketching the broad outlines of the religious history of humanity, I have had but one object; I have wished to show the men of my generation why I remain religious, Christian, and Protestant. I am religious because I am a man and do not desire to be less than human, and because humanity, in me and in my race, commences and completes itself in religion and by religion. I am Christian because I cannot be religious in any other way, and because Christianity is the perfect and supreme form of religion in this world. Lastly, I am Protestant, not from any confessional zeal, nor from racial attachment to the family of Huguenots, although I thank God daily that I was born in that family, but because in Protestantism alone can I enjoy the heritage of Christ—that is to say, because in it I can be a Christian without placing my conscience under any external yoke, and because I can fortify myself in communion with and in adoration of an immanent Deity by consecrating to Him the activity of my intellect, the natural affections of my heart, and find in this moral consecration the free expansion and development of my whole being.

Under this new form, divested of the swaddling-clothes by which at first it was bound, Christianity always seems to me to be best as it is, a spiritual and eternal principle, which brings peace to the soul, and which alone can give harmony and unity to the world. Nothing can contradict it except evil and error; everything serves and strengthens it. It is this principle which to my eyes manifests itself with ever-growing clearness in that heroic love of Science which, in our time, has created so many marvels and made so many martyrs; this it is which reveals itself to me in the works of all the great artists, in that ideal of beauty which enraptures them and brings such generous tears into our eyes; it is this which I honour and bless in the efforts of men who interest themselves in the future of humanity, and who in the political direction of their country or in the work of social education seek and find some means of raising and ameliorating the condition of the people : I salute it in the illustrious apostles of all great causes and in the obscure workers at all humble tasks, from the mother who teaches her children to join their hands and bend their knees before the Father in

Heaven, to the preacher and the missionary who faithfully distribute to the hungry soul the bread of the Gospel, from the sister of charity who devotes her life to the solace of the sick and suffering, to the thinker who fathoms the mysteries of the heart and of the universe in order that he may shed on the paths of erring humanity some rays of light and joy.

Amid the twilight that envelopes us you predict the threatening night; I see the day that is about to dawn with a new century. Where you see nothing but discords, conflicts, and confusion, I see a concourse of forces which, coming from all points of the horizon, are still ignorant of each other, and, because ignorant, conflicting, but which, by these very conflicts and collisions, are labouring together in the common work of elevation and salvation: the mysterious work whose nature Christ defined in His Gospel, and whose motive-power he created by breathing into the human heart His own fraternal love. Since then there has been a secret inquietude at the heart of all egoisms, a sentence of condemnation on the brow of all abuses and all tyrannies. The modern world can never settle down again into repose, or fall asleep in evil and in slavery; it has had a vision it cannot forget; it has been touched with a flame that cannot be quenched. Many who are often the best collaborators in this work of redemption know not whence it comes and whither it tends; they even blaspheme the Christ who inspires it and the God who maintains it. They know not what they do, nor what they say : in their ignorance they calumniate that which is best both in their life and in themselves.

BOOK THIRD

DOGMA

CHAPTER I

WHAT IS A DOGMA?

1. *Definition*

DOGMA, in the strictest sense, is one or more doctrinal propositions which, in a religious society, and as the result of the decisions of the competent authority, have become the object of faith, and the rule of belief and practice.

It would not be enough to say that a religious society has dogmas as a political society has laws. For the first, it is a much greater necessity. Moral societies not only need to be governed; they need to define themselves and to explain their *raison d'être*. Now, they can only do this in their dogma.

Dogma therefore is a phenomenon of social life. One cannot conceive either dogma without a Church, or a Church without dogma. The two notions are correlative and inseparable.

There are three elements in dogma: a religious

element, which springs from piety ; an intellectual or philosophic element, which supposes reflection and discussion ; and an element of authority, which comes from the Church. Dogma is a doctrine of which the Church has made a law.

All the peoples of antiquity believed that their legislation came from heaven. In like manner all the Churches have believed, and many of them still believe, that their dogmas, in their official form, have been directly given to them by God Himself. The history of evolution, political and religious, has dissipated these illusions. Every law of righteousness and truth should, doubtless, be referred to the mysterious action of the Divine Spirit which works incessantly in the spirits of men ; but, in its historical form, it bears, nevertheless, the stamp of the contingent conditions in which it is born. The genius of a people is nowhere more manifest than in its constitution and its laws, nor the soul and the original inspiration of a Church than in its dogmatic creations. The work always bears the moral impress of the workman.

It follows that a Church cannot claim for its dogma more authority than it possesses itself. Only a Church which is infallible can issue immutable dogmas. When Protestantism sets up such a pretension, it falls into a radical contradiction with its own principle, and that contradiction ruins all attempts of this kind.

In Catholicism the theory of the immutability of dogmas is opposed to history; in Protestantism it is opposed to logic. In both cases the affirmation is shown to be illusory. It is with dogmas, so long as they are alive, as it is with all living things; they are in a perpetual state of transformation. They only become immutable when they are dead, and they begin to die when they cease to be studied for their own sakes—that is, to be discussed.

Dogma, therefore, which serves as a law and visible bond to the Church, is neither the principle nor the foundation of religion. It is not primitive; it never appears until late in the history of religious evolution. "There were poets and orators," says Voltaire, "before there was a grammar and a rhetoric." Man chanted before he reasoned. Everywhere the prophet preceded the rabbi, and religion theology. It may be said, no doubt, that dogma is in religion, since it comes out of it; but it is in it as the fruits of Autumn are in the blossoms of Spring. Dogmas and fruits, in order to form and ripen, need long summers and much sunshine. The best way to describe their nature will be to trace their genesis.

2. *The Genesis of Dogma*

Dogma has its tap-root in religion. In every positive Religion there is an internal and an external element, a soul and a body. The soul is inward piety, the movement of adoration and of prayer, the divine sensibility of the heart; the body consists of external forms, of rites and dogmas, institutions and codes. Life consists in the organic union of these two elements. Without the soul, religion is but an empty form, a mere corpse. Without the body, which is the expression and the instrument of the soul, religion is indiscernible, unconscious, and unrealised.

Which of these two elements is primitive and generative? The answer is not doubtful. Modern psychology has learnt it in a manner never to be forgotten from Schleiermacher, Benjamin Constant, and Alexander Vinet. The principle of all religion is in piety, just as the principle of language is in thought, although it is not possible now to conceive of them as being separate. Consider a moment. That religion which time and custom have transformed, perhaps, into a mechanical round of ceremonies, or into a system of abstractions and metaphysical theories, what was it at first? Trace it to its source, and you will find that these cold blocks of lava once came burning hot from an interior fire.

But this is the parting of the ways. This is the point at which religious minds separate into widely different groups.

Regarding religion as a saving institution in the form of a visible organised Church maintained by God and provided with all the means of grace, Catholicism was bound to end in a sort of mechanical psychology, and to explain the sentiment of piety as the inward effect of the outward and supernatural institution. This is done by Bellarmine and de Bonald, the most consistent of the Catholic theologians. Protestantism, on the contrary, which makes of the faith of the heart, of the immediate and personal relation of the soul to God, the very principle of justification, and of all religious life, was bound none the less logically to end, by analysis, in a more profound psychology, and to refer to an inward principle all the forms and manifestations of religion. Religious history thus becomes homogeneous, and runs parallel with that of all the other activities of the human mind.

None the less, this subjectivity of the religious

principle frightens many good men. Persons devoted to practice, and unconsciously dominated by the habits and necessities of ecclesiastical government and religious teaching, hesitate to enter upon a road so naturally opened. As, from generation to generation, religion has been taught and propagated externally by the Church, the family, or special agents, it is impossible for them to imagine that it was not always so, and not to trace back to God Himself that chain or tradition of external instruction. In which they are certainly right. Their only error, but it is a grave one, is to represent God as an ordinary teacher, the first of a series, who once acted, like the rest of them, upon His pupils from without; whereas God works in all souls, acts and teaches without ceasing through all human masters, and is present throughout the whole religious education of humanity.

Who does not see that to represent things otherwise is to remain in the crudest and least religious of anthropomorphisms? At bottom, these men are afraid of losing revelation, which they rightly judge to be inseparable from the very idea of religion. They object that piety and the awakening of the religious sentiment must have an objective cause, and that that cause can only be a revelation of God Himself. Nothing is more true; but this revelation which is effected without, in the events of Nature or of History, is only known within, in and by the human consciousness. This inward inspiration alone enables religious men to interpret Nature and History religiously. Now, this interpretation is made by their intellect and according to the laws and conditions which regulate it. The religious phenomenon therefore has not two moments only, the objective revelation as a cause and the subjective piety as an effect; it has three, which always follow each other in the same order: the inner revelation of God, which produces the subjective piety of man, which, in its turn, engenders the historical religious forms, rites, formularies of faith, sacred books, social creations, which we can know and describe as external facts. It will be seen what an error they commit, what a mistake they make, who identify the third term with the first, suppressing the second, which is the necessary link and forms the transition between the other two. Whoever will fathom this little problem in psychology, and reflect upon it with a little attention, will see that all religious revelation of God must necessarily pass through human subjectivity before arriving at historical objectivity.

Passing now from the intellectual interpretation to the intellectual expression of religion, and noting the successive stages through which it must necessarily advance towards dogma, I remark once more that man's first language is that of the imagination. The imagination of the child or of the savage animates, dramatises, and transfigures everything. It spontaneously engenders vivid and poetic images. At the beginning, religion, consisting chiefly of emotions, presentiments, movements of the heart, clothed itself in mythologic forms. . . . But the age of individual reflection comes. The image tends to change into the idea. Men interpret, define, translate it. The religious myth is replaced by the religious doctrine. These are at first entirely personal interpretations. Nevertheless, these opinions desire to propagate themselves, to become general, and, as they are imperfect and diverse, they engender conflicts which threaten to become schisms. Myths, appealing to the imagination merely, and only professing to translate the common emotion, draw souls together and fuse them into a real unity; individual reason, private exegesis, inevitably separates them. But the consciousness of the community, thus menaced, naturally reacts by the instincts of conservation. There is therefore a struggle between the two, and out of this conflict dogma is born.

A new element must intervene. There must be a Church. Now, all religions do not form churches. The phenomenon is only produced in the universalist and moral religions. Strictly speaking, there is no Church except in Christianity; and no dogmas save Christian dogmas. In ancient societies, where religion was confounded either with the State, or with the nationality, the religious unity was maintained and guaranteed by the same means as the political unity. There were no dogmas, because dogmas were of no use. As much may be said of Hebraism and of Islam: in them there were rites, external signs and seals, which sufficed to weld and to maintain the religious bond.

Dogma only arises when the religious society, distinguishing itself from the civil, becomes a moral society, recruiting itself by voluntary adherents. This society, like every other, gives to itself what it needs in order to live, to defend itself, and propagate itself. Doctrine necessarily becomes for it an essential thing; for in its doctrine it expresses its soul, its mission, its faith. It is necessary also that it should carry its doctrine to a degree at once of generality and precision high enough to embrace and to translate all the moments of its religious experience and to eliminate all alien and hostile elements. Controversy springs up and threatens to rend it. The Church then chooses and formulates a definition of the point contested : it enacts it as the adequate expression of its faith, and sanctions it with all its objective authority: dogma is born. From that moment also the two correlative notions of *orthodoxy* and *heresy* are formed. Orthodoxy is official and collective doctrine ; heresy is individual doctrine or interpretation. . . . By and by symbols or confessions of faith are formed, and these become the standards of faith and practice in the various churches that adopt them.

This long evolution is fully justified in the eyes of reason. It is a movement of the mind as legitimate as it is necessary. The germ must become a tree, the child grow to manhood, the image be transformed into the idea, and poetry give place to prose. It is possible to be mistaken as to the nature, origin, and value of dogma, but not as to its necessity. The Church may make a different use of it in the future, but it will not be able to dispense with it, for the doctrinal form of religion answers to an imperative need of the epoch of intellectual growth at which we have arrived. No one can either reverse or arrest its development. . . .

The word dogma is anterior to Catholicism. It had two senses in Greek antiquity : a political and authoritarian sense, designating the decrees of popular assemblies and of kings ; this is the meaning which dominates and characterises the Catholic notion of dogma. But the word had also in the schools of Greece an essentially philosophical and doctrinal meaning ; it designated the characteristic doctrine of each school. The Protestant Churches have inherited this latter sense of the word : it is in perfect harmony with the spirit and the principle of Protestantism. Dogma, in the Protestant sense, means the doctrinal type generally received in a Church, and publicly expressed in its liturgy, its catechisms, its official teaching, and especially in its Confession of Faith.[1]

3. *The Religious Value of Dogma*

The intolerance of Catholic dogmatism has

[1] Originally the word dogma signified a command, a precept, and not a truth (Luke ii. 1, and the Septuagint of Dan. ii. 13 ; vi. 8 ; Esther iii. 9 ; 2 Maccab. x. 8, etc.). Ignatius of Antioch still uses the word in this sense. It is not until towards the time of Athanasius or of Augustine that it begins to be used of the doctrinal decisions of the Fathers, the Councils, and the Pope. (Cf. also Acts xv. 28, 29. This is afterwards called a dogma, the only time it is used in the N.T. with reference to a decision of the Church.)

had consequences so revolting, and, in Protestantism, wherever this dogmatism has revived, it has given rise to conflicts so sterile and so lamentable, that certain minds have gone so far as to deny the utility of dogma in the largest sense of the word, and have wished to suppress all doctrinal definition of the Christian Faith. To call dogma either divine in itself or evil in itself is to go to an unwarrantable extreme. In religious development, whether individual or social, it has an organic place that cannot be taken away from it, and a practical importance that cannot be contested.

Religious faith is a phenomenon of consciousness. God Himself is its author and its cause; but it has for psychological factors all the elements of consciousness—feeling, volition, idea. It must never be forgotten that these verbal distinctions are pure abstractions; that these elements co-exist, and are enveloped and implicated with each other in the unity of the ego. In the living reality there has never existed feeling which did not carry within it some embryo of an idea and translate itself into some voluntary movement. . . . As it is impossible for thought not to manifest itself organically by gesture or language, so it is impossible for religion not to express itself in rites and doctrines.

No doubt, in the first period of physical life, sensation dominates, and at the *début* of religious life, feeling and imagination. But as science springs from sensation, so religious doctrine springs from piety. To say that " Christianity is a life, therefore it is not a doctrine" is to reason very badly. We should rather say, " Christianity is a life and therefore it engenders doctrine ; " for man cannot live his life without thinking it. The two things are not hostile ; they go together. In apostolic times the greatest of missionaries was the greatest of theologians. St. Augustine at the end of the old world, Calvin, Luther, Zwingle, at the beginning of the modern world, followed the example of St. Paul. When the sap of piety fails, theology withers. Protestant scholasticism corresponds to a decline of religious life. Spener, by re-opening the springs of piety, renewed the streams of theology. Without Pietism Germany would have had no Schleiermacher ; without the religious revival at the beginning of this century we should have had neither Samuel Vincent nor Alexander Vinet.

If the life of a Church be compared to that of a plant, doctrine holds in it the place of the seed. Like the seed, doctrine is the last to be formed ; it crowns and closes the annual cycle of vegetation ;

but it is necessary that it should form and ripen ; for it carries within it the power of life and the germ of a new development. A Church without dogmas would be a sterile plant. But let not the partisans of dogmatic immutability triumph: let them pursue the comparison to the end : " Except a grain of wheat fall into the ground and *die*," said Jesus, " it bears no fruit." To be fruitful, dogma must be decomposed—that is to say, it must mix itself unceasingly with the evolution of human thought and die in it; it is the condition of perpetual resurrection.

Without being either absolute, or perfect in itself, then, dogma is absolutely necessary to the propagation and edification of the religious life. The Church has a pedagogic mission that could not be fulfilled without it. It bears souls, nourishes them and brings them up. Its rôle is that of a mother. In that educative mission, we may add, the mother finds the principle and aim of her authority, the reason and the limit of her tutelage. In this sense, dogma is never without authority. But this same pedagogic authority is neither absolute nor eternal ; it has a double limit, in the nature of the pupil's soul, which it ought to respect, and in the end it would attain, the making of free men, adult Christians, sons of God in the image of Christ and in immediate relationship to the Father. If dogma is the heritage of the past transmitted by the Church, it is the children's duty first to receive it, and then to add to its value by continually reforming it, since that is the only way to keep it alive and to render it truly useful and fruitful in the moral development of humanity. It is therefore to this idea of necessary dogma, but of dogma necessarily historical and changing, that we must henceforth accustom ourselves; and we shall most easily habituate ourselves to it by tracing its evolution in the past.

CHAPTER II

THE LIFE OF DOGMAS AND THEIR HISTORICAL EVOLUTION

1. *Three Prejudices*

I HERE encounter three prejudices which are, I think, the most inveterate in the world. The first is that dogmas are immutable; the second, that they die fatally the moment they are touched by criticism; the third, that they form the essence of religion, which rises or falls with them. I wish to show that dogmas have neither this pretended immobility nor this delicate fragility; that they live by an inner life extraordinarily resistant and fecund, and that the criticism of dogmas, so far from injuring the Christian religion, frees it from the chains of the past and permits it to manifest its marvellous gift of rejuvenescence and adaptation to circumstances.

The proof that dogmas are not immutable lies in the fact that they have a history. That history is as full of conflicts, controversies, revolutions, as the history of philosophy. . . . One Church has said of its dogmas what a Jesuit General said of his Order : *sint ut sunt aut non sint!* It is an illusion. Momentarily arrested at one point, the movement begins again at another. In one half of Christendom, and certainly the most living half, criticism of dogma has never ceased since the sixteenth century. Even in the bosom of the Catholic Church, its most skilful advocates, the Mœhlers and the Newmans, unable to deny that Catholicism is not to-day what it was in the first centuries, have made this strange concession to history ; they have applied to dogmas the theory of development. At Paris in 1682 the dogma of the infallibility of the Bishop of Rome would have been condemned as an error. Since 1870 the orthodoxy of 1682 has become the gravest of heresies. There is no fiction more evident than that of the immutability of dogmas, whether in the Catholic or in the Protestant Churches. Like all other manifestations of life, they have an evolution as natural as it is inevitable. The proof that dogmas are not religion, and that criticism does not kill them but transforms them, will appear in what I now proceed to say.

2. *The Two Elements in Dogma; and its Historical Evolution*

Dogma is the language spoken by faith. In it there are two elements: a mystical and practical element, the properly religious element; this is the living and fruitful principle of dogma: then there is an intellectual or theoretical element, a judgment of mind, a philosophical proposition serving at once as an envelope and as an expression of religion.

Now, it is not an arbitrary relation which unites and amalgamates these two elements in dogma; it is an organic and necessary relation. Go back for a moment to the origin of religious phenomena, and to the formation of the first and simplest doctrinal formulas. In presence of one of the great spectacles of Nature, man, feeling his weakness and dependence with respect to the mysterious power revealed in it, trembled with fear and hope. This is primitive religious emotion. But this emotion necessarily implies, for thought, a relation between the subject which experiences it and the object that has caused it. Now, thought, once awakened, will necessarily translate this relation into an intellectual judgment. Thus, wishing to express this relation, the believer will exclaim, *e.g.* "God is great!" marking the infinite disproportion between his being and the universal being which made him tremble.[1] He obeys the same necessity which makes him ordinarily express his thought in language. Religious emotion then is transformed in the mind into the notion of a relation, *i.e.* into an intellectual notion which becomes the expressive image or representation of the emotion. But the notion and the emotion are essentially different in nature. In expressing it, and thanks to the imagination, the notion may renew or fortify the emotion, and dogma may awaken piety; but the two must not be confounded. The notion is like an algebraic expression which ideally represents a given quantity, but it is not the quantity itself. This must be clearly kept in mind if we are to avoid the most disastrous confusions. In religion

[1] It might be supposed that I make of this elementary experience the primary root whence all dogmas, including the Christian, have sprung by a process of evolution. Nothing of the kind. This is but a particular example. The revelation of Nature is the principle of the dogmas of the Religions of Nature. Christianity has behind it another revelation and other experiences: the revelation of God and of a higher life, in the historical appearance of Jesus Christ. Let a man morally prepared to hear the Gospel begin to follow Him, listen to His words, penetrate His soul, comprehend His death, and he will cry out: "God is Love!" as the spectator of Nature was supposed to exclaim: "God is great!" And this new proposition, translating a new religious relation, will, in its turn, become the principle of all Christian dogmas.

and in dogma the intellectual element is simply the expression or envelope of the religious experience. . . .

The intellectual will therefore be the variable element in dogma. It is the matter united to the germ, and it is ceaselessly transformed by the very effect of the movement of life. The reason of this is simple. We said just now that a religious emotion, like every other, translates itself into a notion which fixes the relation of the subject to the object, implied in the emotion itself. But what will this notion be? With what materials, with what concepts, will the religious man construct it? Clearly with those at his disposal. His religious formula will depend on his state of intellectual culture. A child, he will think and speak religiously as a child. Religious reason and language have followed the same steps as the general reason. . . .

I am well aware that many Christians imagine that God has revealed to us dogmas in the Bible, and that they will accuse me of denying revelation. God forbid! We believe with all our soul in Divine Revelation and in its particular action in the souls of prophets and apostles, and especially in Jesus Christ. Only, the question is whether the revelation of God has consisted of doctrines and dogmatic formulas. No. God does nothing needless, and since these doctrines and formulas can be and have been conceived by human intelligence, He has left to it the care of elaborating them. God, entering into commerce and contact with a human soul, has produced in him a certain religious experience whence, afterwards, by reflection, the dogma has sprung. That therefore which constitutes revelation, that which ought to be the norm of our life, is the creative and fruitful religious experience which first arose in the souls of the prophets, of Christ, and of His apostles. We may be tranquil. So long as this experience shall be renewed in Christian souls, Christian dogmas may be modified, but they will never die.

But why should we retain dogmas which, in the nature of things, must always be imperfect? Why not have religion pure and simple without dogmas? What would happen if we listened to this cry for pure unmixed religion? By suppressing Christian dogma you would suppress Christianity; by discarding all religious doctrine you would destroy religion. How many great and eternal things there are which never exist, for us, in a pure and isolated state! All the forces of Nature are in this case. Thought, in order to exist, must incarnate itself in language.

Words cannot be identified with thought, but they are necessary to it. The hero in the romance, who was said to be unable to think without speaking was not so ridiculous as was once supposed, for that hero is everybody. The soul only reveals itself to us by the body to which it is united. Who has ever seen life apart from living matter? It is the same with the religious life and the doctrines and rites in which it manifests itself. A religious life which did not express itself would neither know itself nor communicate itself. It is therefore perfectly irrational to talk of a religion without dogma and without worship. Orthodoxy is a thousand times right as against rationalism or mysticism, when it proclaims the necessity for a Church of formulating its faith into a doctrine, without which religious consciousnesses remain confused and undiscernible.

The mistake that orthodoxy sometimes makes is in denying or desiring to arrest the constant metamorphosis to which dogma, like all living things, is subject. So long as they are alive, dogmas have the faculty of changing and evolving. How is their evolution effected? The analogy between dogma and language will help us to the answer. A language is modified in three ways: (1) By disuse, *i.e.* by the disappearance of words whose contents have vanished; (2) by intussusception, *i.e.* by the faculty which words have, without changing their form, of acquiring new significations; (3) by the renaissance of old or the creation of new words, *i.e.* by neologisms.

Nothing is easier than to establish these three kinds of variations in the history of dogmas. Some religious formulas perish from disuse; others acquire a new content; while still others are themselves renewed. Many doctrines that were once alive and prevalent are seldom heard of now; they gradually passed out of use. There is hardly a dogma dating from the seventeenth or the sixteenth century that has now the same signification that it had at the beginning. The new wine that has been put into them has modified the old skins. There are limits, however, to the elasticity of words and formulas. There comes a moment when the new wine bursts the old skins, and when the Church has to construct other vessels to receive it. In this way neologisms spring up in languages, and new dogmas in theology. In the sixteenth century the dogmas of Justification by Faith and of the universal priesthood were resuscitated with a new energy. The verses of Horace, on which I might appear to have been commenting, are eternally true:

Ut silvæ foliis pronos mutantur in annos,

. . . . .

Multa renascentur quæ jam cecidere cadentque
Quæ nunc sunt in honore, vocabula . . .

. . . .

The evolution of dogma is possible; why is it necessary? Simply because the material of which it is composed is in a state of constant flux and evolution. . . . We do not mean to say that everything in the old formulas should be condemned. There are to be found in them many great and excellent ideas which still retain their truth and power. We simply say that there is nothing absolute in them, nothing that may be imposed by authority on Christian thought. It is always with notions borrowed from current science and philosophy that the Church constructs her dogmas. But science and philosophy are continually evolving and carrying dogma in their train. Everything changes, even our manner of thinking. Why do certain things appear absurd or grotesque in the imaginations of the past? Because we have lost the faculty for comprehending them. It is as impossible for us to think in Greek as to speak in Greek. Since the end of the Middle Ages two or three intellectual revolutions have occurred which have profoundly separated us from antiquity and changed the inner and the outer world in which we live. It will suffice to recall them in a few words in order to deepen our sense of the decadence of Græco-Roman dogmatic Christianity, and of the necessity incumbent upon us to reform and renovate it, if only we are strong enough to answer to the call of God.

3. *The Crisis of Dogma*

The first of these revolutions was a religious one. Our specific consciousness as Protestant Christians dates from the Reformation. Now, the Evangelical Reformation of the sixteenth century was the rupture of the tradition of the Church, of which the Dogmatics of the great Councils was the framework and the centre. In breaking the authority of the Church, the Reformers broke up the basis on which those ancient dogmas had been built. In appealing to the Word of God against traditional doctrines, they at least called in question the Dogmatics of the Councils. After protesting against all the infiltrations of pagan manners and superstitions into the morals of the Church, into its organisation and its hierarchy, into its worship and its rites, why should they regard as sacrosanct the ancient philosophy which had entered into the construction of its dogmas?

On the other hand, the Reformation renewed the Christian consciousness by its fundamental doctrine of Justification by Faith. Until then salvation had come through adhesion to the Symbols of the Church and obedience to its commands. Justification by Faith (and faith here means the trust of the heart) freed the Christian from the tutelage of the priesthood and the bondage of Symbols. To maintain that you can only be saved by believing certain theological doctrines, is the same as to say that you can only be saved by doing certain works; it is to add to or to substitute for faith some other condition of salvation. The second principle of the Reformation therefore also shook the ancient edifice; in Dogmatics it substituted the internal principle of Christian experience for the external principle of authority; it made of Christianity a moral life and no longer a metaphysic. Is it not right and necessary to give the new principles of the Reformation a new theological expression? This process has been going on ever since the sixteenth century and can never cease.

The Reformation displaced the centre of the

Christian consciousness. At the same time there began a scientific revolution which displaced the centre of the universe. I speak of that which is connected with the names of Copernicus and Kepler, and which was continued by such men as Galileo, Newton, and Laplace. Modern astronomy, geology, biology, etc., have completely changed the outlines and the horizon of our philosophy, and rendered for ever impossible the popular cosmogonies which, until then, had reigned supreme. And who does not see the bearing of this revolution on our views of Scripture, on its cosmography in particular, and on many of its minor teachings? The traditional doctrines of creation have been greatly modified, as also the doctrines as to the origin of evil, suffering, and death. These discoveries, it is said, have ruined religion, and are destroying Christian faith. Not so. What is being destroyed is the débris of an ancient philosophy. But they do compel us, absolutely, if we would remain in touch with the thought of our age, to modify the formulas by which the Church has hitherto believed that she might render an account of the origin and evolution of the universe.

A third intellectual evolution has been effected in our own time by the advent of the Historical

Method. This has completely upset the traditional view of the history of mankind. Floods of new light have been poured upon the prehistoric and historic races of man. Modern criticism and exegesis have given us an entirely new view of the origin and contents of many parts of the Old and New Testaments. In every department of knowledge the historic method has made the point of view of evolution possible and victorious. It is in vain to oppose it, for it is the law of life. Those who cling to the doctrine of dogmatic immutability, whether in the Catholic or the Protestant Churches, are exactly in the position of the Romish cardinals who covered Galileo with anathemas and protested energetically against the rotation of the earth. Neither their protests nor their anathemas prevented the earth from turning round, and the cardinals along with it. In Protestantism, a resistance so blind would be the grossest of inconsistencies. Dogmatic revision is always alive, both in principle and in fact, in the Churches of the Reformation : in principle, because all Confessions of Faith are relative, and subordinate to the Word of God ; in fact, because the spirit of research, of criticism, and free discussion has never ceased to breathe in Protestant Theology, and breathes to-day more ardently than ever. The work will therefore be completed; I am sure of it. We may lack the faith and courage to carry it on, but, failing us, God will not fail to raise up other fellow-workers with Himself in this great enterprise. Christianity cannot perish; it has never failed to adapt itself to the state of mind of ages past; in the future, it will find and make new forms in which to express and propagate itself, forms adapted to the coming times. . . .

"One day, the monk Sarapion, a man of deep piety and ardent zeal, was told by the priest Paphnutius and the deacon Photinus that God, in whose image man had been created, was a purely spiritual being, without body, without external figure, without sensible organs. Serapion was convinced by the ascendancy of Catholic tradition and by the arguments that had been employed. The assistants rose to render thanks to God for having rescued so holy a man from the wicked heresy of the anthropomorphists. But, in the midst of their devotions, the unhappy old man, feeling the image of the God to whom he had been accustomed to pray vanishing from his heart, was deeply moved, and bursting into sobs and tears, he threw himself upon the ground, and cried out: 'Woe is me! Unhappy man! They have taken away my God. I have no one now to cling to and invoke.'"[1]

Touching image of our own experience and of the experience of humanity! We are always making to ourselves some idol or other. It is very difficult for us to realise that God is spirit: we attach ourselves therefore to some fetish of human fabrication. And then, when science comes and takes it away from us, we are troubled and perplexed, as if they had taken from us God Himself. The study of dogmas and their evolution, were it wider spread, would relieve us of our illusions and calm our inquietude. It would teach us that our religious life depends on our faith alone, and that the God Who is its source and end is independent of all theory or representation, because He is infinitely above all human conceptions, and because, in order never to be separated from Him, it suffices that we worship Him in spirit and in truth.

[1] J. Cassanius, abb. Massil. : Collatio, X. c. III.

CHAPTER III

THE SCIENCE OF DOGMAS

1. *The Mixed Character of Dogmatics*

WE have shown the necessity of a free criticism of dogmas. This criticism, if it is religious, will at the same time be positive; it will tend not to destroy, but to distinguish, in each dogma, that which is truly religious and permanent from that which is philosophical and fleeting. Such is the object of the discipline that, in the schools, is called *Dogmatics*, or the Science of Dogmas. It remains to define its task and to point out the resources which it has at its disposal. Both points are connected with its relation to the Church and to Philosophy. The science of dogmas has always necessarily followed the life of the one and the vicissitudes of the other.

In the religious experiences of the Church it finds the material that it elaborates; from philosophy it borrows the methods according to which it treats this material and the form in which it organises it. This science is, therefore, a mixed science : positive and practical in its object, speculative and theoretical in its procedure, it seeks to connect the religious and moral experience with the rest of the experience of humanity, and to effect the synthesis claimed, in order to their full vigour, by the scientific order of thought and by the moral order of practical life.

This intermediate position of our science, between the Church and philosophy, constitutes its independence and its originality. If, as in Catholicism, it were absolutely subjected to the authority of the Church, and were limited to receiving, without critical examination, its successive decisions and traditions, it would be confounded with the history of dogmas, and would be merely a survival of scholasticism. On the other hand, if it did not start from the data furnished by history and by the personal and collective experience of piety,—if it did not study the Christian life in its objectivity and in its historic continuity, but abandoned itself to purely subjective and general speculations—it would be fatally confounded with philosophy. It escapes this double peril, first, by taking as its object the study of the doctrinal tradition of the Church, tracing it back to its generative principle, following it in its successive forms and necessary evolution; and, secondly, by freely applying to this objective material the principles and rules of a truly rational method, a method that may be avowed as such by philosophers. It thus constitutes the philosophy of religion in general and of Christianity in particular, setting itself to connect the consciousness of the Church with the general consciousness of humanity, and establishing or maintaining between them communications equally profitable to both.

It follows that our discipline, in studying the tradition of the Church, is independent of philosophy. On the other hand, the fact that it borrows its methods and processes from philosophy, renders it independent with regard to the Church. Its freedom springs from its twofold subjection. Such a little principality, placed between two great rival Powers without whose help it could not live, maintains its independence of them both by virtue of their very rivalry, and may become an arbiter, an element of pacification and good understanding, between forces which are only hostile because they either do not know or do not understand each other. Thus the science of dogmas will be free, pacific, fruitful, on condition that it does not break its connection on either hand, but remains in close communication with the two sources of its life, without which it would be liable either to die of inanition for want of food, or of impotence for lack of liberty.

2. *The Science of Dogmas and the Church*

A religious society cannot dispense either with doctrines or doctrinal teaching. The more moral it is in its character, the more it needs a dogmatic symbol which defines it and explains its *raison d'être*. It will have its teachers as well as its pastors and missionaries. The apostle Paul compares the Church to an organism in which each member has its necessary function, according to the special gift it has received. "God," says he, "gave some, apostles; some, prophets; some, teachers" (1 Cor. xii. 28; Rom. xii. 6-8. "Teaching of the Apostles," 13 and 15). In passing through different lips the Gospel takes different forms. It creates divers types of doctrine, divers schools or parties (1 Cor. i. 10-14). It is necessary to instruct the ignorant, to refute heretics, to heal schisms, to administer reproofs, to correct the interpretation of texts. This could only be done by means of discussion, reasoning, exegesis, speculation. It was not an effort of pure science, but of practical science, in the interest of the Church itself, with a view to its inner edification and to the continuous reform of its worship and its faith. The labour of dogmatics thus sprang up spontaneously in the bosom of the Church itself, and it has continued its work, not from without, but from within, through an office which is an essential ministry, an organ of the Church. It could not be done well in any other way. . . .

A religious society, by the very fact that it endures, creates a doctrinal tradition, and this tradition soon assumes a divine character and tends to become an absolute authority. This is the effect of a psychological illusion characteristic of the religious consciousness so long as reflection does not put it on its guard against itself. The object of our faith being divine, we ingenuously transport this quality into the formula by which it has been transmitted to us, and we hold this formula to be divine before we have learnt to distinguish between the essence of faith and its historical manifestations, between the religious substance of the doctrine and its traditional expression. Add to the prestige of the past the necessity of educating the new generations.

Every Christian begins as a catechumen, and, in certain respects, he is and ought to be a learner all his life, for he cannot fail to see that the collective consciousness is always richer and more stable than his own. But, if the aim of Christian education is to produce adult Christians—that is, Christians who, having received the Holy Spirit, have entered into a direct and permanent relation to the common Father, and into personal and living piety, they possess an inward rule of conduct, and along with this a principle of free judgment. As St. Paul says, our tutelage ends when we have attained to our majority. The spiritual man judges all, but is judged of none. He becomes independent of the authority under which he has grown up, as the full-grown man becomes free from the mother who has borne and nourished him. He will, doubtless, always gratefully welcome the tradition of the past; but he feels within himself a higher principle which gives him the right to amend and the power to increase, in some degree, the inheritance he has received from his fathers. No one is either a man or a Christian on any other condition.

The solution of the problem named above is to be found in these considerations. A tradition which desires to be absolute, which misunderstands and stifles individual inspiration, is not only an usurper—it also fails in its mission, which is to make adult Christians, Christians who are inwardly inspired and autonomous. It is like those tyrannical mothers who, if they could, would keep their sons in a perpetual minority. On the other hand, the children, even when they have attained their majority, should not despise their parents and disdain the counsels of experience and of age. Individual inspiration is apt to lead to self-sufficiency and sectarianism; it loses sight of the link of solidarity which unites the generations, and the social continuity in which alone progress is made in the religious life, as in the life of civilisation. The first defect, the tyrannical usurpation of tradition, predominates in the Catholic Church; the opposite defect, that of the intransigeance of individual convictions and of Illuminism, is the plague of Protestant communities. The truth would be found in a middle course, and in the organisation of a traditional Church stable enough to receive and keep the heritage of the past, large and flexible enough to permit in it the legitimate expansion of the Christian consciousness and the acquisition of new treasure.

To this ideal, Catholicism cannot resign itself without succumbing to death. Protestantism aspires to it without reaching it; and yet nothing is more really in the logic of its principle. No Protestant Church professes to be infallible. Its most solemn Confessions of Faith have only a provisional value. The spirit of reform breathes in it without truce, continually. The principal task of the community, as of the individual, is to amend itself, to advance in knowledge and in virtue. A Church which should exclude this spirit of reform would cease to be a Protestant Church. And, of course, the duty of reform implies the legitimacy of criticism, of an appeal to the Gospel better understood, of a constant effort to bring the real up to the ideal. The only matter of importance is to decide aright on the principle or criterion according to which this criticism shall be made.

Shall it be another dogma? No; not even if it be called a fundamental one such as the authority of Scripture. For this very dogma, formulated by tradition, is therefore human and contingent, and is open to criticism like all the rest. With what then, or in the name of what, shall dogma be criticised? Shall we, with Rationalism, take a moral or philosophical axiom as the criterion? We should then violate the autonomy of the religious consciousness; we should denaturalise religion itself, by subjecting it to an external rule; and Dogmatics, basing its fabric on an alien principle, would produce a hybrid structure that would be rejected by believers and philosophers with equal disdain.

The principle of criticism of Christian dogmas can only be the principle of Christianity itself, which is anterior to all dogmas, and which it is the aim of dogmas to manifest and to apply. Now the principle of Christianity is not a theoretical doctrine: it is a religious experience—the experience of Christ and His disciples through the centuries. It is the Gospel of salvation by the faith of the heart, the revelation of a moral relation, of a new relation, of a filial relation, created and realised between the man who is sinful and lost, and the Father who calls and pardons him. Such is the initial germ from which the whole Christian development has sprung, and by which consequently that development should and can be judged.

This generative principle of the life and of all the dogmas of the Church being laid down, and the distinction established between the ideal principle and its successive realisations, all of them necessarily incomplete, the criticism of dogmas will be effected automatically, without violence, and with fruit. It will be enough to tell the story of the genesis and evolution of each of them. It will then be seen what contingent and perishing elements have entered into it in the course of history. Christianity is an organism whose soul is immortal, but whose body is renewed unceasingly by the fact that its materials are in constant movement, and that they are gathered from the various environments through which it has to pass. The philosophical notions which have served it as a temporary expression, and which are doubly dead to-day, either because civilisation has advanced, or because they were without vital connection with the initial Christian experience, fall from the tree like withered leaves or lifeless branches. As to the others, in which the sap still rises from the mother root, they will be seen to be transformed, to grow and flower from year to year under the same salubrious breath of criticism. Our discipline, religiously faithful to the principle of Christian piety, may often find itself in conflict with the administrative powers of the Church, but never really with the Church itself.

3. *The Science of Dogmas and Philosophy*

If less burning, the problem of the relations of dogmatics to philosophy is perhaps more difficult to solve than the problem just discussed. It has given rise to quite as many controversies. The danger is twofold. On the one hand, there is the pretension of scholasticism, the attempt to absorb philosophy in theology and make it subservient. It is still the pretension of a certain simple Protestant orthodoxy, for which there is no philosophy outside the Christian faith. At the other extreme is the attempt of rationalism to include the Christian religion in general ethics and philosophy. In the first case it is dogmatics which absorbs philosophy; in the second it is philosophy which absorbs dogmatics. But, in both cases, the specifically religious phenomena are lost sight of, the original character of Christian piety is misconceived, and theology, no longer having any special domain, succumbs and vanishes. It is the merit of the Reformation of Luther, in the sixteenth, and of the thought of Schleiermacher and Vinet in the nineteenth century, to have brought out and rendered manifest, among all other psychological phenomena, the character *sui generis* of Christian faith and life, and thus to have assigned to theology an object of study, eminent no doubt, but very special and very circumscribed. A task was thus marked out for theology widely different from that of philosophy—

a task which consists, not in explaining everything in heaven and earth, but, more modestly and usefully, in giving an account of the religious experience of the Christian Church. Saved at once from scholasticism and rationalism, dogmatic theology may therefore build itself up in its own domain by the side of the other sciences without menacing or fearing any of them.

Its relations to philosophy will become clear if we call to mind a very simple distinction. Philosophy to-day comprises two parts very different in nature: a study of the thinking subject, or, as it is sometimes called, a critique of reason, or a theory of knowledge; in the second place, a doctrine on the essence and the necessary relations of beings, a metaphysic, or a theory of the universe.

It is easy to see that all the positive sciences are differently related to these two parts of philosophy. None of them, for instance, can dispense with the first, with the criticism of our faculty of knowing and of our means of reasoning, under penalty of mistaking the worth of its own hypotheses, and even the regularity of its processes. It is clear that a physicist cannot dispense with correct syllogisms or with vigilance against illusions of the senses and other errors of method.

But, on the other hand, no savant would accept the yoke of any metaphysic whatever which should come to him *à priori* to dictate to him its conclusions. Upon indications of this nature he desires to form hypotheses and make new experiments; but, as a savant, he will never pronounce before that supreme and decisive consultation of facts.

It is exactly the same with the relations of dogmatics to philosophy. It will have recourse to it for all that regards the theory of knowledge in general and the theory of religious knowledge in particular. Like every other science it needs to ascertain the scope of its instrument in order that it may be under no illusion as to the worth of the work it accomplishes. But also, like every other science, it has the right and the duty to challenge and neglect all general metaphysic which, flowing from another principle than that of the Christian religion, would dictate to it articles of faith or rules of morality.

Let it not be said that every theory of knowledge soon begets a metaphysic in its own image. We know theories which deny the very possibility of metaphysics, and it is a question whether a truly Christian dogmatic accommodates itself to it better than any other theory. It may be maintained in fact that the act of faith which is the expression of the conservating energy of the ego and the principle of all religion is accomplished all the more freely when there is no knowledge, properly speaking, there to hinder it. A common prejudice requires that we should have metaphysics as a support to religion. It is on religion, on the contrary, that metaphysics and ethics rest. Man did not become religious when he heard that there were gods; he only had the idea of God and believed in Him because he was religious. Mystery was the natural cradle of piety. Faith is much less an acquisition of knowledge than a means of salvation and a source of strength and life. It is one thing to speculate on the universal problem; it is another to place one's self by the heart in a living relation of trust, of fear, or of love to the mysterious Being on whom all other beings depend. Religion may possibly be under the necessity of ending in a metaphysic, but a metaphysic does not necessarily end in religion, for there are some kinds of metaphysic which either exclude religion or render it impossible.

A theory of religion, dogmatics can have no other starting point than religious phenomena themselves. From this concrete and experimental principle, from this state of soul produced by the immediate feeling of a necessary relation to God, the entire system should spring and develop. What is not in religious experience should find no place in religious science, and should be banished from it.

It would only be to its detriment, then, that the science of dogmas should throw away its liberty by espousing beforehand metaphysical theses or the final conclusions of any philosophy whatsoever. These theses, springing from another source than religion, have no right, in that religion, to become articles of faith. Rational truths not born of religious feeling would be in dogmatics so many dead weights and heterogeneous elements, which would lead to the greatest incoherence. To build up a professedly revealed theology on a professedly natural one is to construct a system without either unity or profound connection. Such a dualism of principles is as intolerable to science as to piety. Instead of dogmatics subordinating itself to metaphysics, metaphysics ought to include dogmatics as well as the results of all the other sciences.

It is altogether different with the criticism of our means of knowing. In every order of science it is mere levity of mind to commence or to conclude researches a little general without having first determined the precise conditions of real knowledge. The absence of a philosophical critique of this nature explains why savants, so rigorous in their special studies, show a philosophical *naïvety* so great in the conclusions that they draw from them, and so readily crown their discoveries by a pseudo-metaphysic that they impose upon the multitude with all the authority and prestige of science. More than any others, theologians are guilty of this abuse when they wish to make their science the sum of universal knowledge. They would be more soundly religious were they more modest and more reserved. An excellent means of putting ourselves on our guard against this illusion and its deplorable consequences will be to institute, without further delay, a rigorous criticism of religious knowledge. This task, I believe, has never been seriously attempted in France. It is, however, as indispensable to the right conduct of the mind as it is fitted radically to cure us of our dogmatic pride and to inspire us with tolerance and humility. This will be the object of the following chapter.

CHAPTER IV

CRITICAL THEORY OF RELIGIOUS KNOWLEDGE

He who says consciousness says science, or at least, the beginning of science. Consciousness implies a representation. In other words, no modification of the ego becomes conscious except by awakening in the mind a *representative* image of the object that has produced it and of the relation of that object to the ego. All our sensations and all our feelings are accompanied by images. The religious sentiment does not attain to the light of consciousness in any other way. It is because it is a state or conscious movement of the soul that it becomes, it also, a principle of knowledge.

No kind of mental life begins with clear and abstract ideas. An idea is derived from an image, and, in order to produce the image, an external or an internal impression is necessary. It is true that the idea or the image has, in its turn, the mysterious power of reproducing and renewing the sensation or the feeling from which it sprang. On this is based the art of teaching and the power of tradition. But this must not be allowed to produce in us the illusion that originally the idea preceded the sensation. The development of the mental life of children is proof of the contrary. We only know that by which we or our kind have been in some degree affected. Our ideas are simply the algebraic notation of our impressions and movements. That which is outside our life is outside our view. Without the external sensations which represent the action of the world on the ego, we should have no knowledge of the world. Without the subjective reaction of the ego against that action of the world, a reaction which manifests itself in the moral, æsthetic, and religious life of the soul, we should have no moral or religious idea, no notion of the good or the beautiful. All our metaphysical ideas come from that source.

It remains, of course, to inquire what is the worth of ideas of this order. It is the particularly complex and delicate question that we here approach. There is no serious philosophy to-day that does not start with a theory of knowledge. Religious knowledge cannot escape by any special privilege. The criticism of it is all the more necessary, because illusion, in this matter, is so easy, and because it clothes itself in a sacred character. The theologian who undertakes the scientific treatment of dogmas without first measuring the scope of the instrument he employs, and estimating the worth of the materials he uses, knows not what he is doing.

1. *Obsolete Theories of Knowledge*

Formerly three explanations of our knowledge prevailed in philosophy: the hypothesis of a primitive revelation; the idealist theory; and the sensualist theory.

The first was revived three quarters of a century ago by de Bonald and Joseph de Maistre. It no longer needs to be refuted. According to this hypothesis, our ideas came to us, not from within, from the naturally productive force of the mind, but from without, by way of supernatural communication. This communication from God consisted at the outset in the gift to man of a perfect language. The exact word brought with it the right idea. "Man," said de Bonald, "thought his speech before speaking his thought." If errors have crept in and reigned among men, it is because they were not able to preserve without corruption the sacred deposit of that primitive language and philosophy. Is it necessary to show how thoroughly this theory is contradicted by psychology and history? It is said that in certain countries there still exists a Botany, according to which the Great Spirit, having created the trees of the forest, comes in the night each Spring to stick the leaves and blossoms on the branches. The immediate communication of right ideas and supernatural virtues to man in his infancy implies a contradiction; it forces us to imagine in him thoughts prior to the action of his intellect and virtues previous to the action of his will. Lastly, it is to misconceive the nature of the mind to make of it something passive and inert. The mind is the thinking and willing force—that is to say, a force productive of thoughts and volitions. If it is not this, it is nothing. We must affirm, no doubt, that God creates this force and directs its evolution, but it is a contradiction to say at once that He creates it and that it is unproductive. It cannot exist without being productive. It is of its very essence to produce. Mind is only mind in so far as it is a force that produces thought and volition.

The aim of this hypothesis, moreover, was to found the divine authority of an infallible tradition by making it go back to the earliest times. These revealed ideas, by the very fact that they are the ideas of God, have an absolute and eternal value. Man finds them guaranteed in the religious caste, to which the deposit has been confided, and which has preserved them intact. Thus arose the idea of an infallible authority. So they say. But the idea of dogmatic authority never appears in early times; it is of very late date; it is elaborated very slowly, according to a psychological law that we have already discovered. Everywhere, and in the traditions of all religions and Churches, it appears after all other doctrines as the keystone which closes and binds together the arch. It is an ultimate dogma logically derived from other dogmas, and afterwards used as a warrant for them. Such was the dogma of Papal Infallibility promulgated at the Vatican Council of 1870; such, in Protestantism, was the dogma of Biblical infallibility, completed by the theologians of the seventeenth century. To base the value of religious notions on a supernatural authority, with a view to rendering them indisputable, is a vicious circle; the authority, it is evident, is the product of these notions themselves. All systems of authority end by shutting themselves up in this circle and perishing in it.

The idealist theory of the origin of ideas is but the philosophical form of the preceding one. It also is an endeavour to trace back our general ideas to the divine understanding as their primary source. Pure ideas, type-ideas, according to Plato, constitute the intelligible Cosmos of which material phenomena are but the unreal and ephemeral shadows. Clearly to conceive these divine ideas is to reach the transcendent reality of things—it is to possess true knowledge. From Platonism to the realism of scholasticism, from this to the geometry of Spinoza and the dialectic of Hegel, the form of the theory has varied constantly; the substance of it has remained the same. Hegel always said : " The rational is the real," and, for him, as for Plato, absolute knowledge resolved itself into perfect logic.

Pyschology has long since dispelled the scientific illusion of idealism. We do not wish to recall the pitiful failure of all the attempts formerly made, and even in our own times, to deduce *à priori* the laws of the physical world. Everywhere, in this domain, the method of observation has superseded the deductive method. The reason of it is simple. An idea, however lofty, can only give out what it contains, *i.e.* other ideas. We know very well that our ideas are in our mind, but they are only in it in the state of ideas. How do we know that the objects which they represent exist outside ourselves? Only by logic can we pass from the idea of a thing to the external reality of that thing. Experience is necessary. Without it our ideas are empty forms. One may conjure with them for ever without ever reaching anything objective. They are shells without kernels. Pure idealism, so far from furnishing a solid theory of knowledge, ends in scepticism, *i.e.* in the negation of knowledge.

The excesses and failures of idealist theories of knowledge have always given rise in history to the opposite theory of sensualist nominalism, according to which our ideas are simply transformed sensations. Unhappily, sensualism, in laying down this axiom, never explained the nature and still less the cause of that marvellous transformation. "There is nothing in the understanding," said Locke, "that was not previously in the senses." To which Leibniz rightly replied: "Except the understanding itself;" that is to say, the force which from sensation draws knowledge. By suppressing this ideal principle, you remove from science all element of necessity—that is to say, all general worth. With Hume, the sensualist theory, so far from giving an account of knowledge, ended in pure phenomenalism, *i.e.* once more, in scepticism. It is, in fact, with isolated sensation as with pure idea; you may press it as much as you will, you will never get out of it anything but what it contains—that is to say, contingencies without any connection between each other. Materialism is still more embarrassed to furnish any theory whatever of knowledge, for it does not even succeed in explaining sensation. Between a mechanical movement and a phenomenon of consciousness there is an impassable abyss. One of the most evident marks of the inferiority of the philosophy of French positivism is that it has not even approached this problem of knowledge, and that it has been able to constitute itself without any other than popular psychology.

2. *The Kantian Theory of Knowledge*

Thinkers may to-day be divided into two classes: those who date from before Kant, and those who have received the initiation and, so to speak, the philosophical baptism of his critique. These two classes of minds will always have much ado to understand each other. The first are dogmatists or Pyrrhonists. The second no longer comprehend either dogmatism or Pyrrhonism. For them, the point of view has been displaced.

Thanks to Kant, we judge both our knowledge and our faculty of knowing; we give an account to ourselves of the conditions in which it performs its functions, of the forms which determine it, and of the limits that it cannot pass. Kant compared, without exaggeration, the revolution which he effected in philosophy to that which the discovery of Copernicus effected in the system of the world. In philosophy also the sun has ceased to move round the earth, and the ancient illusion has been vanquished and dispersed. The idea and the reality no longer coincide; they are disjoined. The intelligible no doubt is real; but it is not certain that all the real is intelligible. Reality appears to us now as surpassing not only our knowledge, but our means of knowing. The religious notion of mystery has entered into consciousness. Man has attained to intellectual humility. Like his body, his mind is a mean between the infinitely great and the infinitely little, between nothing and everything. The deductive philosophy of the unity and necessary and continuous unfolding of an eternal substance, gives place to the philosophy of observation, which will be found to be that of the antinomies whose permanent conflict produces the ascensional progress of the world and of life.

To make Kantism end in scepticism shows a lack of intelligence. His system enables us, on the contrary, to form the *scientific* theory of science. The truth is to be found neither in dogmatism nor in Pyrrhonism, both of which Pascal combated with equal vigour. In modern science there is a certitude invincible to the subtlest Pyrrhonism; but there is also in it a sense of the limits of our knowing faculty and of the relative character of our most solid constructions which forbids man ever to be puffed up to the point of believing himself to be God. To be in this mean is to be in the truth. The same critique which establishes the validity of human knowledge lays down the limits beyond which it cannot go. We have come to know ourselves better, and that is the mark of all true progress in philosophy. *Know thyself* is always its first rule and its final fruit.

The Kantian theory of knowledge, while satisfying the mind, at the same time sets forth the essential antinomies whose normal play constitutes the very life of the ego and explains its multiple manifestations.

There are two elements in all knowledge: an *à posteriori* element which comes from experience, and an *à priori* element which comes from the thinking subject. The first is the *matter* of knowledge; the second is the *form*. Separate, these two elements are unproductive. With the first alone we have but a reality not known; with the second alone we have but a knowing without reality. Their union renders them mutually fruitful by organising the data of experience into the necessary forms of thought. The principle of causation, *e.g.*, is not in things; it is in the mind, and it is the mind which spontaneously connects all phenomena. Science, at bottom, consists in nothing but the causal connection of things. Where the chain breaks, positive knowledge ends. This clear sense of ignorance on points on which we really are ignorant is still a part of science and one of its principal forces, for it proves that it knows itself very well, and also knows the conditions apart from which it no longer exists. But, whether triumphant or held in check, positive science can neither renounce its task and method nor modify their nature. It can only seek to complete, or rather to lengthen, the chain of phenomena. The success of this ever-identical effort, an effort always in the same direction, is what is called its conquests and its progress. It follows that the irresistible tendency of science will be to extend over the whole of the phenomena the ever-tighter network of an invincible necessity. Determinism is its last word.

On the other hand, the ego which knows is an acting ego. Its thought itself, properly speaking, and this display of science, are only one of the forms of its inner activity. It wills, and it must will. If the world acts on it by sensation, it acts incessantly on the world by its volitions. And let it not be said that the will simply represents a mechanical reaction of the ego, exactly equivalent to the action of the external world upon it,—that it is a simple transformation of energy,—for this is not true. Without here raising the question of liberty, it is certain that I do not give back in will simply what I have received under the form of sensation. I deliberate on the motives which urge me to act; I choose between them; I feel myself under obligation; I feel that I should will the good. It is impossible to conceive of moral action without the idea of end. I conceive it, therefore, under a different form from that of mechanical action. Responsibility and obligation are not less the necessary forms of will than logical necessity is the necessary form of thought. But soon there arises in man the most tragical of conflicts. Scientific determinism renders moral activity unintelligible, and moral activity comes into collision with the determinism of science. If mechanical determinism be absolutely true, my will is null; I am simply an automaton. If my responsibility is real, if my personal energy is not an illusion, there is in the world something besides matter, and, for man, there are other than mechanical laws. Thus divided in myself, I ought not to practise what I know, and I cannot do what I ought. I remain floating between a science which is not moral and a morality that I feel to be unscientific. My intellect destroys my will. As the one develops the other dies. The better I know the laws of the world the less reason I have for living and acting. My morality, at each act, gives the lie to my science, and my science, at each affirmation, refutes my morality. Such is the deep malady, the spiritual misery, of the best of our contemporaries. They feel that, with them, vital energy is in inverse proportion to the extent and penetration of thought. It is then that they declare that pessimism, a radical pessimism, is the truth; that existence, will, desire, are the chief evils, and that the supreme effort of science should be to cure us of them by delivering us from all our illusions; after which, in its turn, it will be extinguished itself, like a flame that has consumed the food on which it fed.

Still, the conscious subject is *one*. You cannot proclaim it vain without at the same time proclaiming the vanity of its ideas as well as of its efforts. The ruin of morality draws after it the ruin of science. Moreover, the conflict of which we speak is different from a theoretical contradiction whose solution may be indefinitely postponed. The conflict is practical; it is of the vital not of the intellectual order. It is an internal dissolution of the being itself, a struggle between its elementary faculties, in which the mind is weakened, droops, and dies.

The solution, therefore, if there be one, can only be a practical one, a solution springing from the will. What is needed is to give the mind confidence in itself. It is necessary to increase the energy of its inner life in order that it may find the strength to believe and to affirm in face of the universe the sovereignty of spirit. This is the same as saying that the solution of the conflict is religion; not an external religion, doubtless, in whose hands the thought and will of man should abdicate—that would in no wise re-establish their inner and living harmony—but an inward religion, an activity of spirit which grasps in itself the supremacy of the universal spirit, and by an act of intimate confidence, an instinctive impulse of the being ready to perish, affirms to itself its own dignity, and makes to spring up out of its own substance the irresistible religion of spirit. Thus the conflict of the theoretic reason and the practical reason eternally engenders religion in the heart of man. Let us show more clearly still this necessary genesis of religion.

In observing, in reasoning, in generalising, I arrive at a certain knowledge of that which surrounds me; this knowledge of external objects forms within me the contents of what I call my knowledge of the world. On the other hand, in acting, in living, in exercising my will, is formed what I call my knowledge of myself. Consciousness of self, and consciousness of the world, condition and determine each other, and cannot exist without each other. But, at the same time, they enter into mortal conflict. The ego desires to master the world, and the world, in the end, devours the ego. Thought triumphs over Nature and contemns it; Nature takes its revenge and swallows up thought in its abyss. The consciousness of self wishes to bring over to itself the knowledge of the world; and this absorbs and devours the consciousness of self. The synthesis and reconciliation can only be found in the consciousness of something superior to self and the world on which both of them absolutely depend. This synthetic and pacificatory consciousness is the consciousness of universal and sovereign Being; it is the sense of the presence of God. To escape from his distress, man has never had any but this means of salvation. The savage has recourse to it, according to his degree of intellectual life, when, under terror of the phenomena of Nature, and of ever-threatening death, he calls to his aid the obscure power of his gods. The philosopher, nourished on speculation, and arrived at the dualistic and divided consciousness of the disciples of Kant, obeys the same instinctive impulse and the same vital necessity when he seeks in the notion of God the conciliation of the conflict which he feels between the ego and the world, between pure reason and the practical reason. He needs a universal Being on whom he feels himself to depend, and on whom he may equally make to depend the whole universe. In uniting himself to Him, he affirms and confirms his own life; he feels God to be active and present, in his thought under the form of logical law, in his will under the form of moral law. He is saved by faith in the interior God, in whom is realised the unity of his being. It is therefore true to say that the human mind cannot believe in itself without believing in God, and that, on the other hand, it cannot believe in God without finding Him within itself.

That is a *salto mortale*, some superficial spirits will say, astonished at an apparent deduction which thus makes the religious activity of the ego spring from the depths of its own distress and despair. To which we respond: it is, on the contrary, a *salto vitale*, the instinctive and at the same time reflective act which moves the mind to affirm to itself the absolute value of spirit. Considered at this first psychological moment of its birth, the religious faith of spirit in itself and in its sovereignty is only the higher form, and, as it were, the prolongation of the instinct of conservation which reigns in all Nature. The mind, crushed beneath the weight of things, stands up and triumphs in the feeling of the eternal dignity of spirit.

Inward religion, sacred instinct of life, divine, immortal force which necessarily appears at the first movement of spirit, how they misunderstand thee who only see in thee the slavery of man! On the contrary, it is thou alone that breakest all the chains that Nature binds on him, that savest him from death and from extinction, and that openest out to his beneficent activity an infinite career by associating him with the work of God: it is thou that renderest his spontaneity creative, that renewest his forces, and that, plunging him into the fountain whence he issued, maintainest in him an eternal youth!

This issue to the conflict of our faculties is exclusively of the practical order; it is an act of trust, not a demonstration; an affirmation which presupposes, not scientific proofs, but an act of moral energy. This act must be performed, or we must die. There is no constraint except the desire to live, but this is irresistible, if not for each individual in particular, at least for mankind in general. The individual may commit suicide; humanity desires to live, and its life is a perpetual act of faith.

Nevertheless, this practical solution implies the possibility and the hope of a theoretical one; and this in two ways: in the first place, psychologically, because the ego of pure reason is also that of the practical reason and feels itself to be one and the same knowing and acting subject; then, speculatively, because in believing in the sovereignty of spirit in ourselves and in the world we affirm that man and the world have in spirit the principle and the aim of their being. In God present in us, are reconciled, at least in hope, the ego and the world. This religious faith of spirit in itself permits us to anticipate the future solution, and to affirm that at the summit of their complete development, and in their entire perfection, science and the moral life will rejoin and penetrate each other. Mathematicians tell us that two parallel lines meet in infinity. So in God are reconciled the pure reason and the practical reason, which here seem to us to develop themselves on parallel lines without ever being able to meet and to unite. Let us never forget that we spring out of nothingness, or, if you will, out of unconsciousness, and that we slowly emerge into the light of consciousness. Man is in course of being made spirit. If it be well considered, it will be seen that this irreducible antithesis that fills us with despair is the very condition of our spiritual development. The mind only disengages itself from the bonds of its mother, Nature, by an incessant struggle. Struggle means opposition and victory. Experience demonstrates that nothing spiritualises, deepens, or purifies morality more than the contradictions of science; and finally, that nothing helps science more than a high and disinterested morality. These two sisters, enemies in appearance, are twins, and they are seen to grow and triumph together by the exercise they give to each other through their constant contradictions.

.   .   .   .

3. *The Two Orders of Knowledge*

... The ego can only be conscious of itself and of its modifications. That which does not touch it in any way remains unknown. Now, the modifications of the ego may be reduced to two groups. The one comes to it from without, representing the action of things upon it; these are sensations. The other springs up within, representing the action of the ego on things, its spontaneous energy, its volitions, and its acts. Thence come the two constituent elements of every consciousness, the distinction between object and subject, the ego and the non-ego, thought and the object of thought. We call *objective* every idea or quality that it is possible to refer to the object alone, independently of the action or disposition of the subject. We call *subjective* all knowledge implying identity of subject and object, all discipline bearing on the rules of the spontaneous activity of the ego, since without that activity the rules which should direct it would not exist. In the first case we are conscious of a distinction and even of a radical opposition between the object and the subject of knowledge; in the second, we are conscious of their fundamental identity in this sense, that the thinking and willing subject presents itself to itself as an object of thought and study. In order that the two orders of knowledge, engendered by this duality of origin, may be brought into logical unity, it is necessary either that the subject should enter into the object, that the ego should be absorbed by the non-ego, so that the laws of the non-ego should become the laws of the ego—and that would be materialism; or that the object should enter into the subject so that the laws of the subject should become the law of things—and that would be idealism. Outside these two systems, equally violent and absolute, the two orders of knowledge are irreducible, because in us the consciousness of the ego and the consciousness of the world are at present in conflict. Morality is neither reconciled to science, nor science to morality. In their *rapprochement*, progressive to infinity, a hiatus always subsists.

One would be greatly deceived if he reduced this difference to the ordinary opposition between the physical and the spiritual, between external and internal phenomena. Sensation, the foundation and the starting point of the objective order of knowledge, is just as internal as volition. On the other hand, man is a part of what we call Nature; and, as such, he is the theatre of a crowd of internal and external phenomena which, so far as that is possible, should be observed, described, explained, by the principle of causality, like all the other phenomena of the physical order. For example, the mechanism of memory and that of logic, the correlation between mental activities and the physiological modifications of the cerebro-spinal system, the laws of association of ideas, the stable forms of the human understanding, all that psychology that is now called "scientific psychology," rightfully enters into the domain of the sciences of Nature. It is a province that may be explored like all the others. The psychological observations made in it are objective not less than those of physiology, for the reason that the phenomena that are observed, while occurring in the ego, are nevertheless produced in it without the voluntary intervention of the ego, and even without its express consent. Moreover, they do not imply or provoke on the part of the ego any moral judgment properly so called.

On the other hand, take the sciences of Nature which deal with the objects most widely removed from man, with astronomy or geology, *e.g.*; no longer consider the bare external results; consider rather that spiritual force which we call thought, and which has the virtue of producing these sciences; what are they but the external revelation of the creative and organising energy of the thinking subject, the revelation of spirit to spirit? The work, seen from this subjective side, serves simply to set forth the worth of the worker. You speak then of the ordinary savant or of the intellectual genius, of the good or bad scientific workman. The philosophy of science becomes a necessarily subjective discipline. "Science," in fact, is simply an abstraction. In the reality there are only minds more or less ignorant, conscious, at each step, of their strength and of their impotence, of their defeats and victories,—minds condemned to a perpetual effort to struggle out of the night from which they slowly mount. When you think of this most disinterested side of the scientific life you ask yourself what is the basis, in the last resort, of this confidence of mind in itself—the foundation of all the rest. You see clearly that this activity of pure intellect demands, like all other human activity, attention, forgetfulness of self, a heroism, in short, going to the point of contempt of common enjoyments and of the sacrifice of life itself. You have then left the domain of the sciences of Nature and have entered the realms of spirit, and there rise around you the problems which form the object of the moral disciplines.

Such is the intimate complexity of the two orders of knowledge that a persevering reflection discovers them to be everywhere mingled, and it is with difficulty that they are disentangled. All knowledge is an aggregate (*ensemble*) of judgments; but the judgments which constitute physical knowledge and those that constitute moral science are not of the same nature. The first are judgments of *existence*, bearing solely on the causality, the succession, the distribution of phenomena, *i.e.* on the relations of objects to each other, apart from the subject. The basis on which they rest is sensation, and, as sensation has for necessary forms time and space, time and space will also be the forms and limits of these judgments. Forming homogeneous quantities, time and space give the notion of figure and of number, so that mathematics is the foundation and the necessary framework of all the physical sciences. They rise above this abstract science of the forms of sensibility in the order of their complexity, and form a hierarchy from rational mechanics to sociology, of which

Comte and so many others vainly endeavour to make a simple social mechanics. The destiny of this universal objective science is to progress for ever without ever being completed; for it is of the same nature as number—that is to say, essentially indefinite and imperfect. It not only finds an inexhaustible subject of study in the external world; it encounters a mystery impenetrable to its methods and analyses in the very subject that creates it, and which, in creating it, remains outside the mechanism it sets in motion.

In fact, when the thinking subject considers itself, or considers things in relation to itself, it brings to bear upon itself and them a second series of judgments of an altogether different character. It estimates them and it estimates itself according to a *norm* which is in itself. It declares them to be good or bad, beautiful or ugly, rich or poor in life, harmonious or discordant. In other words, it is no longer the idea of number—it is the category of *the good* which becomes the necessary form of these new judgments, which, for this reason, are called judgments of *estimation* or of dignity, and it is clear that between these two kinds of judgments there is no common measure. They can no more encounter each other than two balls rolled on different planes.

Will it be said that the judgments founded on the concept of *the good* are insignificant and worthless because neither man nor the good of man can be the measure of things? If this remark is useful for abating human pride and preventing childish illusions, it does not efface the primordial distinction between good and evil inherent to the human mind, nor would one wish to deduce from it the vanity of all morality, and the equal worth of all the manifestations of life. The proof, moreover, that the rule of *the good* is above man is that it judges and condemns him pitilessly; it is that consciousness, independently of the painful or agreeable sensations that it receives from things, establishes between them a fitness (*convenance*), a hierarchy, and constitutes the harmonious unity of the universe itself in the supreme idea of the sovereign good. If the legitimacy of the confidence which the conscience has in its rule is to be contested, I do not see why we should not contest that of the confidence of pure thought in itself. Then everything crumbles to pieces, both science and conscience, in the same abyss.

In reality, the good, the beautiful, the relations of fitness and of harmony, are so many principles of knowledge, which progress, like physical knowledge, by the culture of the mind. The form of the moral judgments is universal, and identical in every man; it is this form alone which constitutes man as a moral being; but the contents of this form vary unceasingly in history, according to times and places. Everywhere and always man has sought the good, but he has not always placed it in the same things; he has formed different ideas of it, and these ideas have become more and more noble and pure in proportion as his life itself has been ennobled and purified. That is why there is a history of morality, of religion, of æsthetics, as there is a history of the natural sciences, although progress in these two classes has been of an opposite nature and accomplished according to different laws. However this may be, we may conclude that if mathematics, by the concept of number, the abstract form of sensation, is the mould and framework of the sciences of Nature, ethics, by *the categorical imperative*, the abstract form of the activity of spirit, is the foundation of the moral sciences, which are as diverse as the various activities of the ego, each having special rules and criteria, no doubt, but always falling under the common form of obligation.

Distinct and often in conflict, these two orders of knowledge are none the less *solidaire;* they are always developed by their action the one upon the other, and tend to a higher unity, the need for which gives rise to attempts, renewed from age to age, at a metaphysical synthesis. If you take the disciplines as taught in the schools to-day, you will find that they are almost all mixed sciences such as history, social economy, politics, philosophy, etc. So soon as the savant rises above the simple description of phenomena, and wishes to organise his cosmos by formulating the unity and harmony of it, he necessarily borrows this principle of organisation and of harmony from the experience of his subjective life. On the contrary, religion, art, morality, can only be realised in the conditions prescribed to them by science properly so called, and the last problem always propounded to human thought at each stage of its development is the conciliation of the *moral idea* acquired by the exercise of the will, and the *scientific idea* furnished by its experience of the world.

There is no question, then, of separating the two orders of knowledge, but of referring each of them to its true source, and preventing a confusion which, mixing everything up, renders everything uncertain. It is impossible in good psychology to trace to one centre the divergent manifestations of our spiritual life, and to drive the moral into the physical or the physical into the moral. Our spiritual life is like an ellipse with two centres of light: on the one side, the centre of *receptive life*, where all the sensations received are elaborated into phenomenal knowledge; on the other, the centre of *active life*, at which are concentrated all the revelations of the mind's own inner energy. The line of the ellipse described by the relation and the distance of these two centres is the approximate but never perfect synthesis of the two kinds of data which thus arrive in consciousness. He who does not distinguish these two centres, and transforms the ellipse into a circumference with equal rays and an unique centre, necessarily remains in chaos and old night.

From these general considerations is naturally deduced the specific character of religious knowledge, its inward nature and its range.

4. *The Subjectivity of Religious Knowledge*

The first contrast that we have seen to arise between the knowledge of Nature and religious knowledge is that the first is *objective*, and that the second can never pass out of *subjectivity*. This does not mean that the second is less certain, but that it is of another order, and is produced in another way and with other characteristics.

In one sense, the knowledge of Nature is subjective, for it depends on our mental constitution, and on the laws of our knowing faculty. But religious and moral knowledge is subjective in a different manner and for a deeper reason. The object of scientific knowledge is always outside the ego, and it is in knowing it as an object outside the ego that the objectivity of that knowledge consists. But the object of religious or moral knowledge—God, the Good, the Beautiful—these are not phenomena that may be grasped outside the ego and independently of it. God only reveals Himself in and by piety; the Good, in the consciousness of the good man; the Beautiful, in the creative activity of the artist. This is only saying that the object of these kinds of knowledge is immanent in the subject himself, and only reveals itself by the personal activity of that subject. Absolutely eliminate the religious and moral subject, or rather take from him all personal activity, and you suppress, for him, the object of morality and religion.

Let us take up again that striking antithesis of the two orders of knowledge. What is at once the basis and the sign of the objectivity of the natural sciences?

One may theoretically ask whether the world

of science, the world that *appears* to us, is exactly the real world, existing outside of us. It is thus that in the philosophy of Kant the famous question as to *the thing in itself* is stated. But it is equally certain that in the name of that philosophy this question ought logically to be discarded. One is astonished that the author of the *Critique of Pure Reason* did not immediately close that door opened to scientific scepticism. After his critique, in fact, it is evident that that substratum which some are forced to imagine as a support to phenomena—that the indeterminate and indeterminable substance that they represent beneath the forms and qualities of things,—is both a non-being and nonsense. *Das Ding an sich ist ein Unding.* (The thing in itself is an unthing.) It is a remnant of ancient metaphysics which ought to be eliminated from modern philosophy. In allowing it to introduce itself into our theory of knowledge, it overturns it as would a heterogeneous element. He that persists in distinguishing between the thing in itself and the phenomenal thing will never be able to give an account of the objectivity of the sciences of Nature, and of the kind of certitude that belongs to them.

That which appears to us from without is not

doubtless all the reality of the world; but it is a real world. By his calculations, Leverrier came first to suspect the existence of a large planet as yet unperceived; then he came to measure its volume, to trace its orbit, and finally to mark its place at a given time. He said to his brother astronomers: "Look there!" and the planet appeared at the end of their telescopes.

How explain, moreover, without this reality of science, the power that science gives to man over Nature? His power, is it not always exactly in proportion to his knowledge?

In what then does this objectivity of science consist if it is not founded on the pretended knowledge of the thing in itself? In the necessary link that scientific thought establishes between phenomena. This necessity does not come from experience, for it is something ideal, which our mind adds to all experience. But, as we can only think according to these necessary laws, we necessarily objectivise in all scientific study. We thus affirm, of necessity, the fundamental unity of the laws of thought and the laws of phenomena. Experience always confirms this immediate affirmation. Now this necessity, it is objectivity itself; it is the only noumenon that we are authorised to seek behind phenomena in

Nature, and behind the manifestations of pure reason in spirit.

The first effect of this objective necessity is to eliminate from the work of science the feelings and the subjective will of the ego. A thinking and acting subject is no doubt necessary in making science; but the characteristic of science is to see what it studies apart from the subject, apart even from the psychical phenomena that it observes in the ego itself. Posited outside the ego, the laws that it promulgates appear to us therefore independent of it. This elimination of the subject from the conclusions of science thus becomes the sign and the measure of their objectivity. Where the elimination is complete, as in astronomy and physics, the objectivity is entire. On the contrary, history, *e.g.* where the elimination can never be absolute, always tends towards objectivity, but never reaches it.

It is altogether otherwise with religious knowledge. With it we enter at once into the subjective order—that is to say, into an order of psychological facts, of determinations and internal dispositions of the subject itself, the succession of which constitutes his personal life. To eliminate the ego would not here be possible; for this would be both to eliminate the materials and to dry up the living spring of knowledge. An ancient illusion pretended that we know God, as we know the phenomena of Nature, and that the religious life springs from that objective knowledge as by a sort of practical application. The very opposite is true. God is not a phenomenon that we may observe apart from ourselves, or a truth demonstrable by logical reasoning. He who does not feel Him inside his heart will never find Him outside. The object of religious knowledge only reveals itself in the subject, by the religious phenomena themselves. It is with the religious consciousness as with the moral consciousness. In this the subject feels obliged, and this obligation itself constitutes the revelation of the moral object which obliges us. There is no good known outside that. The same in religion: we never become conscious of our piety without—at the same time that we feel religiously moved — perceiving, more or less obscurely, in that very emotion the object and the cause of religion, *i.e.* God.

Observe the natural and spontaneous movement of piety: a soul feels itself to be trusting, that it is established in peace and light; is it strong, humble, resigned, obedient? It immediately attributes its strength, its faith, its humility, its obedience, to the action of the Divine Spirit within itself. Anne Doubourg, dying at the stake, prayed thus: "O God, Do not abandon me lest I should fall off from Thee." The prophet of Israel said: "Turn me, O Lord, and I shall be turned." And the father in the Gospels cried: "Lord, I believe; help Thou mine unbelief." To feel thus in our personal and empirical activity the action and the presence of the Spirit of God within our own spirit, is the mystery, but it is also the source, of religion.

It will be seen how much religious knowledge and the science of Nature differ by their very origin. The one is the theory of the receptive and logical life of the ego; the other is the theory of its active and spontaneous life. As both the receptive and the active life are one, however, the two orders of knowledge are neither isolated nor independent. But they must never be confounded. Their results will always remain heterogeneous; they are not of the same order, and cannot supply the place of each other. If you were to admit, *e.g.*, that philosophers may succeed (as they have often been believed to do) in establishing a veritable objective science of God, and if they were thus to know God in Himself and apart from the religious ego, that scientific knowledge of God, even if it were possible, would not be religious knowledge; for to know God religiously is to know Him in His relation to us—that is to say, in our consciousness, in so far as He is present in it and determines it towards piety. This is the sense in which it is permissible to maintain that religion is as independent of metaphysics as it is of cosmology. It is the same with the knowledge of the world. To know the world as an astronomer or a physicist is not to know it religiously. To know it religiously is, while taking it as it is, and in no wise contradicting the scientific laws according to which it is governed, to determine its value in relation to the life of spirit; it is to estimate it according as it is a means, a hindrance, or a menace, to the progress of that life. In the same way, to know ourselves religiously is not to construct scientific psychology; but that psychology being once constructed, and properly constructed, it is to realise ourselves in our relation both to God and to the world, forcing ourselves to surmount the contradictions from which we suffer, in order that we may attain to unity and peace of mind. Thus, not only can religious knowledge never cast off its subjective character; it is in reality nothing but that very subjectivity of piety considered in its action and in its legitimate development.

The inner nature of these two orders of knowledge having been defined, it becomes evident that each of them is valid in its own domain, and that they cannot legitimately encroach upon each other. To try to establish by religious faith the reality of any phenomenon whatsoever, of which experimental science or intellectual criticism are the sole judges; or to wish to formulate by means of objective science a moral judgment which springs from the subjective consciousness—these are two equivalent encroachments and abuses. Experimental science has the right to forbid the religious consciousness to do violence to it; but the religious consciousness has an equal right to restrict science to its true limits. We must prevent confusion if we would put an end to the conflicts between them. To enclose God in any phenomenal form is, properly speaking, superstition or *idolatry;* to confine or dissipate the soul in external phenomenism, and to deny the seriousness and value of its religious and moral activity, is *infidelity*, properly so called.

Truths of the religious and moral order are known by a subjective act of what Pascal calls *the heart.* Science can know nothing about them, for they are not in its order. In the same way, the phenomena of Nature are only known and measured by observation and calculation. Neither the heart nor religious faith can decide with respect to them. Each order has its certitude. We must not say that in the one the certitude is greater than in the other. Science is not more sure of its object than moral or religious faith is of its own; but it is sure in a different way. Scientific certitude has at its basis intellectual evidence. Religious certitude has for its foundation the feeling of subjective life, or moral evidence. The first gives satisfaction to the intellect; the second gives to the whole soul the sense of order re-established, of health regained, of force and peace. It is the happy feeling of deliverance, the inward assurance of "salvation."

It is not surprising, lastly, that these two kinds of knowledge or of certitude should spring up and propagate themselves by different means. Objective science transmits itself by objective demonstration. The subjective life of the savant has nothing to do with it. To convince us of the reality of his discoveries, an astronomer does not need to be a good man. On the contrary, a fundamentally immoral man will always be a detestable professor of ethics. Religion is only propagated by religious men. It may also be added that, in religious knowledge, the intellectual demonstration or the idea has no value except in so far as it serves as the expression and the vehicle of the personal life of the subject. This is the secret and the mystery of eloquence. The *si vis me flere, dolendum*, is true in all the moral disciplines, as much and more than in æsthetics. One gains nothing by attempting to demonstrate objectively the existence of God. That demonstration is ineffective towards those who have no piety; for those who have, it is superfluous. The true religious propaganda is effected by inward contagion. *Ex vivo vivus nascitur*. Accuracy in theology is much less important in religion than warmth of piety. Pitiful arguments have in all ages been followed by admirable conversions. Those who are scandalised at this have not yet penetrated into the essence of religious faith.

For want of this clear and frank separation between our two orders of knowledge, one sees, on the one hand, philosophers pretending to transform ethics and philosophy into objective science, and, on the other, savants naïvely giving forth their objective science as a metaphysic and as a solution of the enigma of life. Two illusions, in whose train everything is mixed up and confounded. Objective ethics are everything you could wish—except ethics. You might as well speak of a round square. When an objective science transforms itself into metaphysics, it ceases to be science and becomes subjective philosophy. This goes without saying.

And yet, in distinguishing the two orders we must not isolate them, nor above all must we lose sight of their solidarity, their close connection, and correspondence. The subject is one, and has a clear consciousness of his unity; that is why he always tends towards a synthesis. Phenomenal science cannot complete itself without borrowing from the subjective consciousness of the ego the ideas of unity, of plan, and of harmony. On the other hand, the moral and religious consciousness, in order to express itself, needs to borrow from phenomenal science the data which it uses, and, consequently, it should always avoid contradicting them. Thus we tend towards the synthetic harmony of a continuous effort and of an indefectible faith; but we discard none the less resolutely the philosophy of logical unity. We obstinately refuse to admit that the subjective order can ever be deduced, by way of consequence and application, from the objective order of knowledge: that is the error of materialistic Pantheism;

and, *vice versâ*, that the objective order of phenomenal science can or ought to be deduced from the religious or moral order : that is the opposite error of all the dogmatisms. The mental cannot be simply reduced to the physical, or the physical entirely to the mental. We must respect the fruitful antinomies of life from which the necessary progress springs. The tendency towards harmony is there, not the harmony itself. This is the reward promised, the aim proposed, to effort. Our philosophy ought to regard the spiritual life in its becoming—that is to say, in its growth and in its conflicts, without wishing, like all idealist and materialist speculations, to make of the actual and transient moment the eternal metaphysical reality.

5. *Teleology*

Subjective in essence and origin, religious knowledge is *teleological* in its procedure, and this second characteristic springs from the first.

Teleology is the form of all organic life and of all conscious activity. Now, what is moral knowledge but the theory of the conscious life of spirit?

Without the principle of causation, phenomena, in science, would not be connected ; without the idea of end, or principle of direction, biological and psychical facts could not be organised—that is to say, hierarchised.

Mechanism and teleology: these then are the two new terms for the antithesis formed by the knowledge of Nature and religious knowledge. But it is a prejudice to believe that the one form of explanation excludes the other or renders it superfluous. We have examples to the contrary not only in the machines constructed by man, but also in all living organisms, in which, according to Claude Bernard, the *directive idea* of life is realised in an absolute determinism.

The mechanical explanation of phenomena and the determinism of science only become exclusive of teleology when they are transformed into metaphysical materialism—that is to say, when it is affirmed, *à priori*, and by a subjective act, that there is nothing in the universe but matter and the movements of matter. But then, it is clear that materialism, which believes itself to be scientific, becomes a philosophy, and like all other philosophies it falls under the jurisdiction not only of the objective science of the world, but of the consciousness of the ego.

The ideas of cause and end spring from one and the same source. The idea of cause awakens in us because the ego, as soon as it knows itself, has the clear sense of being the author of its acts; it has this sense by that of the very effort that it has made. But, at the same time, it knows that it made that effort with a view to an end which attracted it. Cause and end, therefore, are the two aspects of the same conscious act. The one is the backward glance of the consciousness; the other is its forward look. As we only know the world by reflecting it in the mirror of our consciousness, it follows that the two categories of cause and end impose themselves on our understanding with an equal necessity.

There is another consequence of this psychological observation. The consciousness of the ego is one; neither the idea of cause nor the idea of end, by itself, would suffice to explain the whole universe to me. It is easy to see at a glance that the objective science of phenomena is not and never can be completed. The chain into which it introduces each particular phenomenon as a new link is indefinitely lengthened by scientific progress, in time and space, but without the power to hang on anywhere. Outside space and time, the principle of causation only engenders insoluble antinomies. Besides, to explain one phenomenon by another is to explain it by a cause which itself needs explanation. The mechanical reason of things is therefore never a sufficient reason. It is an indefinite series of insufficient particular reasons. The network of science, however fine and firm it be, does not cover, and cannot cover all reality. The Cosmos that science builds is like the globe; it floats in immensity. "Where, O Lord, goes the earth through the heavens?"

To this question teleology alone responds. But every teleological affirmation respecting the universe is a religious affirmation. Science, studying only accomplished facts, never establishes anything but phenomena and their antecedent or concomitant conditions. Once the phenomenon is integrated in the causal series, the task of science is accomplished. To ask it to go further is to ask it to go beyond its limits and to denaturalise itself. You can only put teleology into the universe by affirming the sovereignty of spirit. To say that there is reason, that there is thought, in things—that they move towards an end or realise an order, a harmony, a good: this is to say that matter is subordinate to spirit. Now, to affirm this sovereignty of spirit is to commit that act of initial religious faith of which I spoke at the beginning; it is to feel in one's self and in the world something besides matter, the mysterious energy of spirit. This act of faith—legitimate because inevitable—belongs to the subjective order of religious life, not to the objective order of science.

Teleology and the theory of final causes have been compromised because their specific character has been mistaken; they have sometimes been assimilated to, and sometimes substituted for, mechanical causes in the explanation of phenomena. For an unknown scientific explanation has been substituted an appeal to a supernatural intention or volition of God. The savants rightly protested against this. God, who is the final reason of everything, is the scientific explanation of nothing. The object of science is to search for second causes; where these do not appear there is no science. It is faith which replaces it. To say that God created the world, or that the world tends toward the sovereign good, is not to advance positive science a single step. On the other hand, to explain the phenomena of rain, or thunder, or the fall of bodies, is to dissipate some mythological conceptions; but it is not to suppress the religious affirmation of spirit that the mechanism of the universe has an end, and that the laws of gravitation and the material forces serve some purpose of which they are ignorant, and which is of more value than themselves.

Between the discoveries of science and the postulates of the religious and moral life there is always necessarily formed a synthesis which is destroyed at each step, but which rises again higher and larger than before. Mechanism itself, in order to be intelligible, calls for teleology. The text of the material world awaits the interpretation that spirit gives of it. By its discoveries positive science establishes the text. Without this rigorous establishment of the text, the exegesis of consciousness remains a phantasy. But, without that exegesis, the text itself signifies nothing; it is almost as if it did not exist.

There is another reason, a practical reason, which makes of teleology the very essence of the religious consciousness. We must never lose sight of the fact that what we seek in and by religion is the key to the enigma of life. The enigma of the universe only torments us, at the religious point of view, because we believe that in this is the secret of that. We are embarked in the vessel, and we see clearly enough that our destiny depends upon its own. That is why religious faith, perfectly indifferent to the architecture and to the ways and means of the construction of the vessel, regards above all the direction in which the sails are set, and seeks to discover the route which is being followed. Has it a compass? And is there some one at the helm?

In other words, the religious instinct is the pressing need that spirit has to guarantee itself against the perpetual menaces of Nature. Faith judges everything from the point of view of the sovereign good, and the sovereign good, for spirit, can only be the final and complete expansion of the life of the spirit. Therefore, in every religious notion there will never, at bottom, be anything but a teleological judgment. It is not the essence of things—it is their reciprocal value and their hierarchy which interest religious faith. In the religious notion of God it is not the metaphysical nature—it is the will of God in regard to men— which is of most concern; and in the religious notion of the world it is not the mechanical cause of phenomena—it is to know which way the world is going, and whether it has any other end to serve than as the theatre and the organ of spirit. What does faith itself desire to say when it defines God as the Eternal and Almighty Spirit, except that man needs to affirm that his own individual spirit does not depend on any but a spiritual power like himself? It is true that to determine this final cause of the world is also to determine its first cause. It is the same thing in other terms; and indeed it is to make metaphysics in the etymological sense of the word. The important point is to know that this decisive step beyond the chain of visible phenomena, whether it be taken by the philosopher or the theologian, is always an act of subjective life, an affirmation of spirit, an act of faith, and not a demonstration of science.

6. *Symbolism*

Thirdly, and lastly, religious knowledge is *symbolical*. All the notions it forms and organises, from the first metaphor created by religious feeling to the most abstract theological speculation, are necessarily inadequate to their object. They are never equivalent, as in the case of the exact sciences.

The reason is easy to discover. The object of religion is transcendent; it is not a phenomenon. Now, in order to express that object, our imagination has nothing at its disposal but phenomenal images, and our understanding, logical categories, which do not go beyond space and time. Religious knowledge is therefore obliged to express the invisible by the visible, the eternal by the temporary, spiritual realities by sensible images. It can only speak in parables. The theory of religious knowledge requires for its completion a theory of symbols and symbolism.

What is a symbol? To express the invisible and spiritual by the sensible and material—such is its principal characteristic and its essential function. It is a living organism, in which we must distinguish between appearance and substance. It is a soul in a body. The body is the manifestation of the soul, although it is not like it; it makes the soul active and present. The most perfect example of symbolism, in this respect, is found in language and writing—two incarnations of thought. Neither the characters formed by my pen, nor the sound made by the air in my larynx, have a positive resemblance to my thought. But these letters and sounds become signs to those who have the key to them. They express the intangible thought; they make it present and living in the minds of those who read or hear.

This is still truer of the creations of art. They also are mere symbols. Art might be defined as the effort to enshrine the ideal in the real, and by a material form to express the inexpressible. This is clearly taught by the word *poesy*, which means creation. The works of great artists really live; for they have a soul, a rich and intense life, which the material form at once conceals and reveals. From architecture to music there is not an art that is not symbolical. Ethics, religion, all the disciplines relating to the subjective life of spirit, have only this means of expression. It is their peculiarity to become exterior and objective, and to dominate the external things that science studies. Symbols, much better than science, attest the victory and the royalty of spirit. If science reveals Nature, symbols make of Nature, of its transformations and its laws, the glorified image of the inner life of spirit.

Born in the artist's soul, of the subjective activity of his ego, the symbol addresses itself much less to the pure intellect than to the inner life and to the emotions of those who contemplate it. It awakes and sets in motion the subjective activity of the ego; it has produced its whole effect when it has produced in us the emotions, the transport, the enthusiasm, the faith, that the poet himself experienced in engendering it. Such is the source and the explanation of "the magic of art," of eloquence, of religious inspiration. All the creators of living symbols pour their soul into our soul, their life into our life. They subjugate and ravish us. By symbols, much better than by scientific notions, the community and fraternity of spirits is realised, and the fusion of souls into a collective consciousness effected; a consciousness which includes all individual minds and tunes them into harmony; the consciousness of a nation, of a church, of humanity. It is not science that rules the world—it is symbols.

Inferior to the exact ideas of science in logical clearness, symbolic forms are superior to them in power and reach. Science is forcibly arrested at the surface of things, at the appearances continually arising in the universe. In it is found neither the principle of energy, nor, consequently, the secret of life, or the key to our destiny. You seek the meaning and the end of your action; you ask for some sufficient reason for living; do you not feel that it is contradictory to address yourself to the science of phenomena, seeing that, from the strictly scientific point of view, phenomena have not in themselves their own *raison d'être?* That which you seek is beyond phenomena, and it is symbols alone that can, not make you comprehend it, but reveal it to you.

Since Nature may become and does become, in

art and in religion, the constant symbol of the inner life of spirit and of its normal development, —since it is susceptible of this perpetual and glorious transfiguration by spirit,—it is impossible not to admit the inner correspondence of the laws of Nature and the laws of conscious life, and to believe in their deep unity. It is, in fact, secret and powerful analogies which rule and inspire symbolical creations. Art and religion are more than conventions; they are revelations of that which is hidden at once in spirit and in Nature, of the principle of Being itself, of the absolute energy which is manifested, parallelly, in the unfolding of the physical universe and of the moral universe. All things cover some mystery; phenomena are simply veils. That is why, by their very destination, they become symbols.

The idea of symbol and the idea of mystery are correlative. Who says symbol says at the same time occultation and revelation. In becoming present and even sensible, the living verity still remains veiled. The same image that reveals it to the heart remains for the intellect an impassable barrier. One may say of it what the poet says of the sense of the infinite, for, at bottom, it is the same thing. "We are restless because we see it but can never comprehend it."

THEORY OF RELIGIOUS KNOWLEDGE

This inquietude is soothed by a clear knowledge of the cause from which it springs. Symbols are the only language suited to religion. We need to know that which we adore; for no one adores that of which he has no perception; but it is not less necessary that we should not comprehend it, for one does not adore that which he comprehends too clearly, because to comprehend is to dominate. Such is the twofold and contradictory condition of piety, to which symbols seem to be made expressly in order to respond. Piety has never had any other language.

In considerations of this kind might be found the explanation of the bond which in the beginning unites religion and art. But we must confine ourselves to our special topic, and proceed to inquire what it is that constitutes the life and power of religious symbols.

It would be an illusion to believe that a religious symbol represents God in Himself, and that its value, therefore, depends on the exactitude with which it represents Him. The true content of the symbol is entirely subjective: it is the conscious relation of the subject to God, or rather, it is the way he feels himself affected by God. Thus when the Psalmist exclaims: "The Lord is my rock"; or "God is a devouring fire"; when the Christ teaches us to say, "Our Father,"—these are not scientific, and in this case metaphysical, definitions of God. What these images simply translate is the relation of absolute confidence, of awe, of filial love, which, by His mysterious action, the Spirit of God creates in revealing Himself in the spirit of man. From these divers feelings spring spontaneously the strong and simple images which translate them, and which, if these subjective experiences are eliminated, have no content and no truth.

From this point of view we may see in what religious inspiration psychologically consists. Neither its aim nor its effect is to communicate to men exact, objective, ready-made ideas on that which by its nature is unknowable under the scientific mode; but it consists in an enrichment and exaltation of the inner life of its subject; it sets in motion his inward religious activity, since it is in that that God reveals Himself; it excites new feelings, constituting new concrete relations of God to man, and by the fact of this creative activity it spontaneously engenders new images and new symbols, of which the real content is precisely this revelation of the God-spirit in the inner life of the spirit of man.

The greatest initiators in the religious order

have been the greatest creators of symbols. Prophecy, in the Biblical sense of the word, has never given divine revelation except in the form of images. And whence spring these images but from the exaltation of the religious life of the prophet which spontaneously expresses itself without? Every other conception of inspiration is anti-psychological.

To the question, Whence come the life and power of symbols? we reply: From the primitive organic unity of the sentiment of piety, and of the image which translates it first to consciousness. It is the organic unity of soul and body. The greater the creative force that engenders the symbol, the stronger is this unity. It constitutes its truth because it constitutes its life. For a symbol, to be living it suffices that it should be sincere, that the feeling should not be separate from the image, nor the image from the feeling. To this cry of confidence in God, "The Lord is my rock," there is no objection, so long as this confidence is really felt, although a rock is a very poor image of God. It follows that the value of a symbol must not be measured by the nature of the image employed, but by the moral value, in the scale of feeling, of the relation in which it places us to God. It is the moral value of this relation which alone makes the intrinsic value of a religion, and which permits us to assign to it its true place in the development of humanity.

The time comes, however, when the image detaches itself from the feeling that produced it, and when it fixes itself as such in the memory. In considering it in itself, reflection transforms the image into an idea more or less abstract, and takes this idea for a representation of the object of religion. But then arises the original discrepancy that we noted at the outset between the object of religion, which is transcendent, and the nature of the phenomenal image by which we attempt to represent it. Hence there is a latent contradiction in every symbolic idea. To get rid of this contradiction the understanding is obliged to eliminate from these ideas the sensible element which remains in them and renders them inadequate to their object.

By progressive generalisation and abstraction, reasoning attenuates the primitive metaphor; it wears it down as on a grindstone. But, when the metaphorical element has disappeared, the notion itself vanishes in so far as it is a positive notion. There are mysterious lamps which only burn under an alabaster globe. You may thin away the solid envelope to make it more transparent.

But mind you do not break it; for the flame inside will then go out and leave you in the dark.

So with all our general ideas of the object of religion. When every metaphorical element is eliminated from them, they become simply negative, contradictory, and lose all real content. Such are our pure ideas of the infinite and the absolute. If you would give them a positive character, you must put into them some element of positive experience. This is what is done when it is said that God is the ultimate energy of things, that He is the creative cause of everything, that He is Justice, that He is Spirit, a Judge, a Father.

Born of the primitive symbols of religion, all our religious ideas will therefore necessarily keep their symbolical character to the end. As is the seed, so is the plant. Dogmatics itself will never be for the religious soul anything but a higher symbolism—that is to say, a form which, without the inward presence of active and living faith, would be worthless. If dogmas may sustain and produce faith, it is still more true that, at the outset, it is faith which produces dogmas and afterwards revives them.

Many good men withstand these conclusions from a rigorous analysis of religious knowledge and of its psychological genesis. Supposing you are right, they say, and that the mental constitution of our spiritual nature confines religious thought to symbolic forms, cannot a supernatural revelation enable us to pass beyond these limits and bring to us religious ideas adequate to their object, and consequently of a pure and absolute truth? This seems to us a very strange desire—that a revelation of God should be effected apart from the conditions of knowledge—that is to say, apart from the forms under which alone it can be accessible to us. Do they not see that the very idea of revelation soon becomes contradictory? If God wished to make us a gift that we could receive, must He not have suited the form of it to that of our mind? Must He not have availed Himself of our ideas and of our language in order to explain to us the nature of His benefits? Now, it is certain that our ideas, as soon as they are transported outside space and time, contradict and destroy themselves, and that we are reduced to the necessity of conceiving and expressing things invisible and eternal by images actual and terrestrial. If God, in speaking to us of His mysteries, used other than these human means, we should not understand Him at all, so that the revelation would no longer be a revelation. And is it not for this reason that when God has desired to reveal Himself to men He has never employed any but men as His organs, and that He whom we name His Son never spoke except in images and parables of the things of the kingdom of God?

No one in fact was fonder and more intelligently fond of this symbolical form than the Christ; He never wished to employ any other. This preference did not arise, as is supposed, merely from the fact that He found it a happy means of popularity to adapt Himself to all minds. He also knew that no language was more natural or more conformed to the moral exigencies of piety. He saw in it an institution ordained by God Himself. And it is the truth. The Parable addresses itself, not to the pure understanding, but to the active faculty of the ego, to "the heart." It appeals to our subjective life; it awakens the religious need before satisfying it. The soul which hears it meditates, and experiences the living content that it contains. On the contrary, the soul that is inert and dead finds nothing in the symbol and receives nothing from it even theoretically, so that it is literally true that the symbolic form, a shining revelation unto some, remains a dull and empty letter for others. It is from this point of view alone that it is possible to understand that other saying of Jesus, so paradoxical to common sense, so rich and just to the eyes of experience and of faith: "To him that hath shall be given; from him that hath not shall be taken away that which he hath." The gift of God comes only to the felt need and the active desire of man.

7. *Conclusion*

The conclusion from all that has now been said is that religious knowledge is subject to the law of transformation which regulates all the manifestations of human life and thought.

As there is disproportion and disparity between the object of religion and its means of expression, it will always be possible and necessary to distinguish, in all its creations, between the form and the substance, the body and the soul. Religious symbolism will therefore always be very variable *de facto*, but subject, *de jure*, to new interpretations.

This variability, however, is not unlimited. It is necessarily confined within limits which, while not easy to define theoretically, are none the less precise and fixed; for the great religious creations are organisms, and every organism carries in itself, determined by its own nature, the exact capacity of its metamorphoses.

In every living organism, in fact, there is a principle of stability and a principle of movement. The identity of a human being persists through all the modifications, internal and external, which he undergoes. So with the language of a people; and so with every historical religion. Its fundamental and regulative principle is the relation it establishes between the soul and God. The form or external realisation of this principle depends, no doubt, on the race, the geographical environment, the historical period. It will vary therefore with these circumstances. But the religious type or organic principle remaining the same, this religion will appear the same throughout the incessant movement of its dogmas, rites, and symbols. This is the very condition of its life. Forms which cannot bend, symbols whose fresh and living interpretation is exhausted, a rigid body that no longer assimilates or eliminates any external element, represent a state of sterility and death, to be followed by a speedy dissolution.

Pious men are right in clinging obstinately to the stability of their principle of piety, but they ought to cling as tenaciously to the renewal of forms and ideas in their religion; for this is the only proof that their treasure has kept its value, and their religious principle its organising virtue. The life of a religion is measured by this power of adaptation and renovation. If Christianity is the universal and eternal religion, it is because its virtuality in this respect is infinite.

. . . . . .

Before I close, let me try to prevent two misunderstandings. In saying that in dogmas we must distinguish the religious substance and the intellectual form, I do not mean that we either can or ought to isolate them from each other, or that we can ever hope to have them separately. Piety is only conscious for us and discernible by others when incarnate in its expression or intellectual image. A religion without doctrine, a piety without thought, a feeling without expression, these are things essentially contradictory. It is as vain to wish to seize pure piety, as in philosophy it is to seek to define "the thing in itself." When we speak of the inward religious fact, then, of pious experience, we do not speak of a bare experience; we speak of a psychological phenomenon, of a precise and, consequently, formulated experience.

In the second place, for religious science, it is not a question of isolated experience, of the experience of a single individual. The material would be too precarious, and the field of observation too limited. The question refers to the individual life in its continuity, and to the life of the religious society considered in its historical development.

A social and universal as much and even more than it is an individual fact, it is in the social life of the species, in organised religious societies, in their institutions, their common worship, their liturgy, their rules of faith and discipline, that religion objectively realises its fundamental principle, manifests its inner soul, and develops all its power. It is only as a social manifestation that it can become an object of scientific study, and that it has need of explanation. Moreover, a religious life which remains hidden in the individual consciousness, which does not communicate itself, which does not create any spiritual solidarity, any fraternity of soul, is as if it were not; it is a mere film of feeling, an ephemeral poetic flower, which has no more effect on the individual himself than it has on the human race.

From these considerations springs a method. The dogmatic treatment of religious knowledge will have for its subject the tradition of the religious society as it is fixed, conserved, and

z

developed in its historic monuments. It will consider that tradition from the symbolic point of view, as the objective revelation of the inner life of the Church, and of its piety. The tradition will then appear not as something dead and immutable, but as a power continuing in ourselves. To grasp this soul in its fruitful continuity and in the perpetual renewal of the external organism; to comprehend them in their living unity; to tell the story of the genesis of dogmas and their endless metamorphoses as a constant and necessary incarnation of the principle that is manifested in them; to follow this uninterrupted chain in history, and prolong it into our own life,—such is the method, at once critical and positive, conservative and progressive, firm in piety and always deferential to science, which critical symbolism enables us to apply to all religious creations.

The error of that form of religious knowledge called *Orthodoxy* is that of forgetting the historically and psychologically conditioned character of all doctrines, and of desiring to raise into the absolute that which is born in time, and which must necessarily modify itself in order to live in time. Impotent to arrest the current of ideas and the movement of minds, it can only establish its rule by political measures, by regulations enacted and applied like civil laws—decisions of popes, bishops, or synods, trials for heresy, dogmatic tribunals. Orthodoxy has lost the sense of the symbolical character of Confessions of Faith, which, however, it still names symbols. Its misfortune and its failing is to be anti-historical.

The error of *Rationalism*, at once the brother and the enemy of orthodoxy, is of the same nature, but it is produced in an opposite sense. It does not lose sight of the imperfect and precarious character of traditional dogmas and symbols; it exaggerates it; but it loses sight of their specifically religious contents. Orthodoxy is mistaken as to the nature of the body of religion; rationalism as to the nature of its soul. Beneath the old traditional ideas it seeks for other ideas, moral or rational ideas, freer from sensible elements, and less contradictory, which it mistakes for the essence of religion. It replaces dogmas by other dogmas which it believes to be more simple, and which it regards as absolute truth. But in giving to religion a rational or doctrinal content, it empties it of its real content, of specific religious experience; it kills faith, which no longer having an object of its own, no longer has a *raison d'être*. It has less liking than orthodoxy for symbolism and for religious creations; it is radically impossible for it to comprehend, and consequently to interpret, them. The chief vice and the misfortune of rationalism is to be anti-religious.

The theory of *Critical Symbolism*, whose broad outlines we have traced, will bring us out of this old antithesis. It shows to us the kind of truth and the legitimacy possessed by symbolical ideas, without ignoring the psychological and historical determinism which rules their form and their appearance. It must not be imagined that, from this point of view, everything becomes fluid and inconstant in religion—that nothing in it can be fixed or permanent. In the progress of his life, man is destined to realise his spiritual nature, to attain to what St. Paul calls "the stature of Christ," in which the religious and moral ideal is realised. This moral stature is a reality, the highest of all realities. We tend towards it without ceasing, and the value of each moment of our inner life is measured by the progress that it marks towards that supreme end. For this inner life there is a *norm* which imposes itself on the consciousness with an imperative necessity, and, consequently, there may be religious symbols which are normal and normative in relation to others. These are the symbols which represent with perfect simplicity and fitness either this ideal end of the Christian life or some of the necessary moments through which the soul passes on the way to it. There are symbols, in a word, such as that of the Heavenly Father, the Kingdom of God, the New Birth, the Effusion of the Holy Spirit, so intimately bound up with our religious life, with its origin, its progress, or its end, which one cannot conceive as disappearing, so long as the spiritual life of humanity exists. All the exclusively religious words of Christ which bear directly on the consciousness are of this number. And it is of them that He was able to say without being contradicted by the ages: "Heaven and earth shall pass away, but My words shall not pass away."

On the other hand, it is no less impossible to ignore the distinction we have made in symbol between substance and form. Now, this distinction opens the door to criticism. The most conservative of Christians confess that men may adhere to a doctrine without having appropriated its religious content; that they may be orthodox without being pious. They therefore make it the duty of every member of the Church to assimilate the contents of the symbol. But how can the duty of personal assimilation be imposed without the right arising to critically interpret the transmitted forms? Is it not a psychological necessity for each believer to bring his inner religious consciousness into harmony with his general culture? What if these syntheses and conciliations are necessarily unstable and precarious because of the constant development of life and knowledge? When a man is walking his equilibrium is destroyed and re-established at each step. It is the very condition of walking.

Symbolism, which thus makes peace in the individual, may also effect it in religious societies. In Catholicism the unity of the Church is only maintained by a central infallible authority and by political means. That authority creates peace by imposing silence. Dogmas only subsist because no one concerns himself with them. Can Protestant communities maintain their unity by the same method? The Catholic method ruins Protestant communities, inevitably, by causing schisms frequent in proportion as their life and thought become intense. The theory of symbolism offers them a more honourable issue. It permits them to combine veneration for traditional symbols with perfect independence of spirit by leaving to believers, on their own responsibility, the right to assimilate them and adapt them to their experiences. They will attach themselves to tradition with all the more sincerity and zeal as each one is able to find in it that of which his religious faith has need. It will be a help and not a yoke. Men will love it; they will defend it as the link between the generations, as a family heritage, as the place where souls of every race and age, and stage of scientific culture, meet and mingle and commune.

APPENDIX

REPLY TO CRITICISMS

BEFORE laying down the pen, I ought perhaps to reply to one or two objections.

The first reproach that has been addressed to me is contained in the words, "Naturalistic Evolutionism." A conception more or less materialistic of the universe is thus attributed to me, according to which, like Herbert Spencer, I should explain all things by the single law of evolution, and end sooner or later by reducing the laws of the moral world to the laws of the physical world, since I make of the first a simple transformation of the second. Need I say that this is the very opposite of my thought? It is true that I like to use the word evolution, and to consider all phenomena in their natural succession. But this is not a metaphysical doctrine; it is a process of study, a method which consists in these two essential rules: to observe each fact as it presents itself; and to observe it in its order, *i.e.* in the conditions in which it presents itself, because a fact only possesses its truth and value in that order and succession. On our planet, moral life emerges slowly and painfully out of organic life. Must we therefore conclude that there is no more in the one than in the other, and that they are of equal value? Certainly not. Both these series of phenomena must be placed in their relations and connections; but the method which makes them known to me gives me no more right to confound them than to separate them, to ignore their differences than to forget their analogies. It shows me, on the contrary, that there is advance, *real* progress from the one to the other; that the first in date has its end in the second; that there is a sort of living and continuous creation, each stage and degree of which reveals new riches and new glories. This is so thoroughly the basis of my religious philosophy that there would be more ground or, at all events, more excuse for accusing me of denying the reality of the world than the continuous action of the Divine Creator.

It is true that the one reproach has not saved me from the other. Both have been addressed to me by persons who have not taken the trouble to reconcile them. The accusation of Pantheism, contradictory as it may seem, has been added to that of Naturalistic Evolutionism. I have been made to appear the blind and docile disciple of an idealism more or less Hegelian, which would annihilate the reality of second causes in order to contemplate in the universe the flux and transformation of a first cause or substance, of which one might either say that it is everything or that it is nothing. But here, again, they lose sight of the character of the method that I follow. It leads me to discover in my consciousness the mysterious and real co-existence of a particular cause, which is myself, and of a universal cause, which is God. That, I repeat, is a mystery impenetrable to analysis, but undeniable by any man who examines himself and enters into the ultimate basis of his life. It is the mystery out of which religion springs by an invincible necessity. Now, as this mystery is posited by me at the very outset of my researches, and maintained to the end, how can they legitimately reproach me with sacrificing either of the two terms which constitute it to the other—the first effect of which would be to dissipate and make impossible my theory of the psychological origin of religion? "In me," said Charles Secretan, "lives some one greater than me"—a mysterious guest whose universal and eternal action I feel beneath the variable phenomena of my empirical activity, to Whom, when I am good, confiding, humble, brave, I always attribute my goodness, my faith, my courage, my humility, as to Him I attribute my whole life.

I cannot comprehend the co-existence of the finite and the infinite; but this duality is everywhere. I observe that in the physical as in the moral world there is, in each phenomenon, a latent force, a sort of potential energy, which raises it and urges it beyond itself. Nature is perpetually becoming, that is to say, in perpetual travail. It is not true that there is nothing new under the sun, and that the future must simply repeat the past. Creation is not yet completed. "My Father worketh hitherto," said Jesus. "It doth not yet appear what we shall be." But the little that I perceive of the Divine work demonstrates to me that it is progressive, that it raises and enriches life at every step, and that this progress accounts exactly for the essential antinomies amid which my reason loses itself and my heart adores. To wish to reduce everything to unity is to turn the kingdom of life into the domain of death. For my part, I have long since renounced what is justly called "the philosophy of identity," that abstract dialectic which, throwing all things back to their point of logical departure, renders perfectly incomprehensible and superfluous the ephemeral development which they have in our consciousness and in history. The painful contradictions observed by Pascal in our moral life, and the insoluble antinomies in our thought unveiled by Kant, always seem to me to go nearer to the bottom of things than the ontological deductions of Plato, Spinoza, and Hegel.

*   *   *   *   *

In this book I have hardly noted any but facts that have been verified in myself and by myself. It is true that I suppose that every reflective reader is capable of finding them and tracing them out in his own personal experience. Those who are able and wishful to re-read my book in themselves, and thus verify my analyses, may perhaps draw some profit from it. Those who read me otherwise will not only lose their time and pains—they will misunderstand at every step the meaning of my phrases and the direction of my ideas. Beneath my reasonings or my images they will put other ideas and other intentions than mine, and they may afterwards, with an apparent good conscience, deduce from them the most terrible consequences. . . . Philosophical language lends itself to all and permits all; and the mischief of it is that it would be useless to desire to prevent these quarrels. New explanations only give rise to new misunderstandings, and simply serve to perpetuate a dispute without interest and without fruit. We can only repeat the saying of the ancient sages of Arabia: *Magna est veritas et prævalebit.*

THE END

www.ingramcontent.com/pod-product-compliance
Lightning Source LLC
Chambersburg PA
CBHW020233240426
43672CB00006B/512